CHASING NORTHERN LIGHTS

Road Dog Publications was formed in 2010 as an imprint dedicated to publishing the best in books on motorcycling and adventure travel. Visit us at www.roaddogpub.com.

Chasing Northern Lights, Chronicle of a Motorcycle Ride from New York City to the Arctic Circle
Copyright © 2022 Miguel Oldenburg
All rights reserved.

ISBN 978-1-890623-84-5
Library of Congress Control Number: 2022934116

An Imprint of Lost Classics Book Company
This book also available in eBook format at online booksellers. ISBN 978-1-890623-85-2

CHASING NORTHERN LIGHTS

CHRONICLE OF A MOTORCYCLE RIDE FROM NEW YORK CITY TO THE ARCTIC CIRCLE

by

Miguel Oldenburg

Publisher
Lake Wales, Florida

For
Gabriela and Mateo

About the Author

Miguel Oldenburg is a Venezuelan-American multi-disciplinary artist whose diverse talents have taken him down numerous adventurous paths. Known as "Motorwolf," he is a long-distance motorcycle rider with a passion for cultural exploration. He has ridden motorcycles across thirty-six countries, with no plans to stop there.

Miguel has been on a lifetime journey of self-expression through different artistic mediums. When he's not travelling on a bike, Miguel is a four-time Emmy Award-winning creative director, working on design and animation projects featured in several major entertainment brands and production agencies. He also has a profound love for oil painting, and his provocative art has been displayed in New York, the city that fostered his creativity and the place he now calls home. As a musician, he recorded and toured with the Latin ska band King Changó (Luaka Bop—Warner Music), played with the hard rockers Camaro Suicide, and experimented as a solo artist, having played many famous international venues.

Miguel has strong ties to his Latino roots, which are infused into everything he creates. Growing up in Caracas, he became attuned to seeing calmness in the chaos, adventure in the mundane, and inspiration in the natural world, a perspective that has shaped his creativity.

To quote Venezuelan writer Rómulo Gallegos, "There are some people that grow old between thinking and doing." Although this is true for many, for Miguel's rebellious mindset creating and getting things done is a disciplined lifestyle. He sees art as a means to inspire, motivate, transform, and connect with the world around him. When he's not working, Motorwolf can still be observed taking life by the handlebars, riding to the edge of the map and back.

Or, in this case . . . from New York to the Arctic Circle.

Contents

THE RIDE

If I can make it there,
I'll make it anywhere

The unmerciful Arctic weather rushed above me, forming a claustrophobic storm in the skies. I saw the road ahead dim into darkness and the gray clouds transform into a polymorphic time lapse. I felt a cold draft flow through the sleeves of my riding jacket, stiffening my spine and raising the hairs on my arms. The violent downpour hit me with brutality, distorting my perception of reality through the helmet visor. I couldn't see the road at all, and each drop felt like a sharp needle piercing my bare neck. All my senses were focused on keeping my motorcycle straight on the road, which went from gravel, to dirt, to thick mud.

I slowed down to a crawl, and for a brief second, I realized I was alone in the wilderness of northern Alaska, far from any form of civilization, and had no other choice but to move forward wrestling the elements. I was holding the motorcycle grips so tight that I could feel the strain on my shoulder muscles. I was afraid to let the handlebar go to wipe my helmet visor; as the bike was unstable, shaking, and sliding all over the rough terrain.

The road suddenly angled at a steep slope and I let go of the clutch, the motorcycle slid down, and I could see the mud being scooped like ice cream by the front fender. My legs and my luggage were drenched, and the air filter was getting clogged by the dirt that slung back with the spin of the wheels. The motorcycle engine began to stutter, and my reaction was to give it some gas to shake her out of the coughing. Immediately, the rear tire spun to my right side. I yelled in panic inside my helmet, and a large stain of breath fogged the inside of my visor. My body was catapulted into the air. I lost orientation, followed by a hollow silence.

A flash of a lightning bolt and the instant sound of thunder shook me up, realizing the storm was right above me. I was lying on the ground covered in mud, facing the ominous clouds, breathing, conscious, but I couldn't feel my left leg. Pushing my torso upwards was a colossal effort, only to see my leg stuck under the bike. I was alone, hurt, and trapped.

I lost the sense of time as I made several futile attempts to lift the 300 kilos of motorcycle. I heard a guttural huff amid the percussive beats of the rain, and my heart instinctively accelerated its pace, pumping blood to every corner of my body. A cold rush of adrenaline burst in my guts when I saw the brown beast appear from behind the shrubs on the side of the road. The bear kept his distance, assessing the scenario. I was an easy prey, hurt and not able to escape, but the unfamiliar shape of the motorcycle was daunting for the grizzly.

Hunger was the decisive factor, and the bear moved towards me. "¡Hijo de la gran puta!" I yelled as loud as I could, repeatedly cursing him in Spanish. The bear seemed to get angrier at the sound of my voice and stood upward with his front claws facing me; the mighty predator looked gigantic from the ground. I knew that was the end of my ticket. I exhaled, resigning to my inevitable fate. The voracious jaws attacked me, suddenly stopping about one minuscule inch from my face. His breath reeked of breakfast burrito. He grabbed me by the hand and gave me a gentle shake . . . then to my disbelief, I saw the beast talk with a neutral voice, "Stand clear of the closing doors please".

What da hell! I woke up abruptly, watching the doors of the subway car close in front of me. Wait, is this the N train? Did I fall asleep again? Shit!

I missed my stop at Times Square for the third time that week. Standing next to me was a tall and overweight guy, wearing an unkempt brown-camo Mets T-shirt, a messenger bag, and large headphones. He had a half-chewed burrito in one hand and was holding the pole with the other. His hand was uncomfortably next to mine. I was still gripping the pole with all my strength.

Yo! that was some trippy stuff . . . you were yelling some nonsense in your sleep . . .

Uh? Yeah well sorry . . . I murmured while moving my hand down the greasy pole. Which stop is next?

I think it's Herald Square

I can't believe this happened again.

Hey, I understood "puta."

Really dude? I replied. completely annoyed, while squeezing my way out of the packed train.

I came out of the train station and fast-paced myself for the ten blocks back to my office on 42nd Street. I walked, navigating the frantic crowds of New Yorkers during rush hour, tourists with selfie sticks, amateur rappers giving their CDs to everyone, and the surreal circus of multiple Hello Kitties, the naked cowboy, a malnourished Batman, and a few Elmo impersonators.

I bumped hard into Cookie Monster, "¡Chinga tu madre!" I heard the Mexican accent cursing from inside the blue fuzzy head, but as true New Yorkers we both didn't give a damn and moved on. I was zoned out and couldn't shake off the thoughts about the subway event and how much it bothered me. It's almost an unwritten city law to not fall asleep on the trains. But I've been having these nightmares at least twice a week. I knew the haunting images of my recurring dreams were a direct consequence of my fears and concerns about "the ride."

Up to this point, I had ridden motorcycles in every state in America but Alaska, and I really wanted to complete all fifty states. So, I declared this was the year I was going to ride my bike all the way to the Arctic and conquer the last frontier.

My office was wedged in between the Sephora store and the McDonalds restaurant on 42nd Street. Every morning I rushed into the building, pushing its large double doors into the vestibule, which trapped the unique local musk of Dior, Big Mac, and homeless urine. In the lobby, I would say "good morning" in a borderline obnoxious Venezuelan volume to the receptionist. As usual, he didn't reply. He would only acknowledge me at the very last minute to ask for my building ID. I had been working there for years, and every day was the same attitude. He would scan me up and down while looking at my identification, giving me that same creepy discomfort I get from Immigration and Customs officers at the airports, confused about my Spanish name and German last name. His attitude only changed at the beginning of each December when he played the "kind" card expecting a holiday tip. From the hand inside my pocket I would flip him a concealed bird and make my way through the lobby.

The elevator doors opened, blowing its now familiar smell of industrial grease, brass wax, and Windex. I pushed the tenth-floor button and walked into my office, closing the doors behind me. I stood by the window, staring at Times Square and the thousand city lights, screens, and signs flashing below me.

I sat down and logged into my computer, typing on the browser's search box "Northern Lights"; I paused right before striking the "enter" key and watched the little typing cursor blink several times . . . before I frantically deleted it all and typed "bear spray" . . . I had no idea what was to come.

THE CHALLENGE

A TRUE AMERICAN

The idea of riding in all fifty states of the United States began to brew in my head many years ago. But let me rewind for a bit to put things in context.

Back in 1994, I was "found" by Betelgeuse, one of the most relevant television and media post-production houses of New York at the time.

It was an ordinary day in Caracas, my native city in Venezuela; chaotic as usual, extremely dangerous, and carrying its morals in a brown paper bag. I was at my desk working on some designs, when the phone rang and there was a guy on the line talking to me in English. We were in the heyday of television production, and they wanted to fly me to New York, all costs paid, just to be interviewed, and for a young Latino graphic artist like me, this was an unbelievable opportunity.

I showed up at their offices on Park Avenue and had my job interview with no other than the president of the company, John Servidio. After about half an hour of talking business, John threw me a curve ball and asked me with a thick New York Italian accent, "So, Miguel . . . in Venezuela . . . how do you rank yourself?" I really wanted that job, so I looked him square in the eye and with blatant nerve I replied, "I'm the best of my country!" John smirked at my confident display of bullshit. I was only twenty-three years of age, with barely a couple years of work experience, yet somehow, he liked me, so he shook my hand and said, "You are hired!"

That night, I got white-girl-wasted with a bunch of Polish tourists in a random midtown bar, and we sang something that phonetically mimicked "Mister Jones" by Counting Crows all night long. Hell! I had a job in New York; I was moving to America!

Living in the Big Apple was fast and exciting. I worked hard for years, not minding being relegated to cover the doomed 6PM to 2AM night shift. I made a conscious effort to adapt to America; I learned at age twenty-four I was a brown person, and based on the medical forms I had to fill out at my doctor's appointments at the time, I learn that being Latino was, apparently, a race and not a culture. I stopped correcting people butchering my name and got used to being called Migooel, meanwhile I learned to accurately say words like "Connecticut" and "rhythm."

And how to forget the one time the entire Art Department of Betelgeuse went to HBO to make an important pitch. We were all excited to show our new concepts for the re-branding of their legendary sport show "Inside the NFL." We entered their offices on Sixth Avenue and met with a full staff of major executives sitting on a long mahogany table, and when my turn came to present, I commanded the crowd, loud and emphatically, to "fuck-us" on the storyboards. I meant to say "focus," but I fell short on smoothing the edges of my Español. The entire room burst into huge laughs, and such and embarrassment made me invest a great deal of effort in learning the proper pronunciation of the word *focus*. I remember my good friend, Beirne, who was the Senior Designer at the time, teaching me to say first "fo" and immediately "kiss" . . . and only the devil knows that up to this day I still think of that formula every time I say the word.

But I was in love and inspired by this city. Art and creativity were the world I lived in. I painted, drew, designed, visited galleries and shows, wrote songs, joined a band, and played my guitar at places like CBGBs, The Continental, Wetlands, S.O.B.'s, and Coney Island High . . . then I got married and had kids. Full stop.

Fast forward to 2009. I was separated. Full stop.

That year I decided to apply for American citizenship. Aware of the many tragic lessons of immigrants in modern world history, I knew it was a smart idea to share the same nationality with my two kids; but fundamentally I felt proud to become part of this nation, which has given so many opportunities for me and my family to grow over the years.

The day I received my citizenship, I went to a military surplus store and bought an American flag, not so much out of some patriotic urge but as a token to remember the significance of that moment. That same day I told myself, "If you are doing this, then be genuine about it; let's make it real." And right then I decided I wanted to travel all across the United States and visit every region, every corner, every state of my new country. I wanted to learn about the people, the traditions, and the history. I craved to taste everything, from a fresh lobster roll in Maine to a nice shrimp po-boy in Louisiana; I wanted to devour a tender rack of ribs at a Texan BBQ and severely punish myself with one of those ridiculously overpriced organic-gluten-free-vegan-non-GMO kinds of salad in Los Angeles.

By taking on this challenge of traveling all fifty states, I knew my connection with this land would be rooted in a deeper understanding of its culture. I would be able to say confidently to anyone that I really knew my country, by the account of my own eyes and first-hand experiences.

So, I declared . . . If I was to be a true American, I wanted to truly *know* America . . . on a motorcycle . . . all of it!

Wait, on a motorcycle?

Well, yes, let me elaborate. My passion for motorcycles started at a young age. It was 1980. I was about nine years old when I walked past the local bookstore in my town and saw this amazing publication cover of a man wearing a colorful suit and helmet, riding a flashy motorcycle. He looked fast, and it was one of the coolest things I had ever seen. It was on the cover of a brand-new encyclopedia that came out that year named *2 Ruedas—La Gran Enciclopedia de la Moto*. Readers had to buy each issue on a weekly basis in order to build every volume of the "2 Wheels" collection. For a kid like me, it meant I had to work hard on my school grades to get the money from my parents for the encyclopedia. I remember flipping through its glossy pages and wondering what it would be to race on top of a Honda, a Bultaco, or a Montesa motorcycle.

As an '80s kid, my imagination ran free. I rode my old Benotto bicycle nonstop around the neighborhood with a piece of cardboard or a juice box stuck on the wheel spokes, to make the bicycle resemble the sounds of a motorcycle, while pretending to be Johnny Cecotto or Carlos Lavado, the laureled Venezuelan champions of the prestigious Motorcycle Grand Prix, worldwide known as MotoGP.

This fascination for motorcycles stayed with me over the course of my life. From when I was a kid, pinning posters of racers and bikes on my bedroom wall, to later in life, having the wild experience of learning how to ride one and becoming a long-distance rider. Let me tell you a bit of that story . . .

THE VIRAGO

THE LEARNING CURVE

It came like a lightning bolt, striking me in my core. My heart raced to the beat of a two-stroke engine, and a rush of serotonin loaded my mind with sudden confidence. I felt significant and intangible, brave and terrified. I had just let go of the clutch of a motorcycle for the first time in my life. I was in motion, standing on the pegs of a Honda XR 250. I felt the air bending in my face, and the parking lot at my old job site became a Magellanic world of possibilities. I had a clear revelation about what I wanted my life to be: being in control of my own destiny and feeling utterly free.

"¡Frena mamagüevo, frena!" my friend, Marco Colantoni, yelled, urging me to stop before hitting the dumpsters and wrecking his bike. I halted the machine and stood there breathing rapidly with an indelible grin on my face. I knew right then that was a transformative moment in my life.

Marco was the guy who gave me the initial basic instructions to operate a motorcycle. It was something like "first gear is down, the rest are up; this is the clutch; these are the brakes; and this is the throttle . . . go!"

As an Italian-Venezuelan, Marco had a strong affinity to the Lazio soccer team, Fellini films, a taste for good food, motorcycles, and loved the MotoGP races. He had a group of friends that rode motorcycles together on weekends and often organized long distance rides. They all wore bandanas and leather vests and owned these kickass looking cruisers. A pack of second-hand Yamaha Viragos, V-Maxes, and Maxims, tuned to sounds I had never heard on motorcycles before and customized with all sorts of leather straps, fringes, chromed parts, and saddlebags.

Around 1992 or 1993, they went on a group ride to La Gran Sabana, in the Venezuelan side of the Amazonia. They cruised through one of the toughest and most unique landscapes of the world and came back with extraordinary stories from their journey, bonded by an exuberant sense of camaraderie. I couldn't believe these machines could go that far, that a man could conquer such distances and dare to challenge impossible terrains on a motorcycle. They had this superhero glow around them, and more than ever, I wanted to be part of that. I needed a motorcycle.

I was obsessed with the motorcycle idea. With the help of an English dictionary, I would read old *Easyrider* magazines I found in some obscure bookstores in my native city of Caracas. I mirrored myself in the pictures I saw in these publications, of guys controlling powerful machines and riding to distant towns while having a good time. The images of their parties, the girls, and the rallies were hypnotic for a young guy like me in his early twenties.

I dreamed of that brief rush of freedom I had at the office's parking lot with the Honda XR again and again, and wondered what it would be like to adventure with a motorcycle to unknown places. A few months later, I put the money together, and Marco helped me find a bike—my first cruiser, a 1989 Yamaha Virago 750.

Like most people, I began slowly riding within my neighborhood boundaries. I practiced getting used to my bike's controls, riding around La Boyera and El Hatillo in Southeast Caracas. Once I got confident with the mechanics of riding, I started commuting every day to work on the bike. Riding to the heart of the city quickly sharpened my skills. Caracas is an outlaw town, where rules are constantly disobeyed, and it's extremely violent. Some traffic lights go on intermittent yellow after dusk, so people don't have to fully stop and risk being robbed at gunpoint at the intersections, so everyone just keeps going. Now imagine the consequences of that for someone on a motorbike.

In such chaos I had my share of accidents, including that one time I was hit from behind by a city bus and was catapulted into the middle of the oncoming traffic on a main avenue intersection. I let go of the bike and rolled, got up in one continuous move, and ran to the curb of the road. I still can't believe how close I was from tragedy. The official rule in those cases is to wait for the transit police to document the accident, but the waiting made the commuting passengers on the bus really agitated, and the mob decided to testify against me, since I didn't want to move the dropped bike. Yes, they yelled intimidating curses at me, claiming it was all my fault. That's how angry that city is. I was lucky; a good soul who witnessed the bus hitting me decided to stick around and told the police the truth.

Circumstances like that put the whole riding experience into perspective. It taught me of the latent consequences of doing it. I understood that every time I threw my leg over the bike, it could be a one-way ride. But my desires for adventure were stronger than those fears and soon got me out riding through my state and beyond. I would pack a T-shirt and a toothbrush and take on weekend rides to La Colonia Tovar, a bucolic German town in the mountains of Aragua, where visitors can sample the taste of the local bratwurst and beers amid a picturesque setting of Tudor houses and people in traditional dirndl and lederhosen outfits. I also enjoyed riding the Caribbean side of Miranda state, just to enjoy a delicious coconut shake called "cocada" by the beach and to let myself go, in tune with the jocular ways of the coastal people.

The Virago let me discover new places on my own. I didn't have to explain myself or compromise with anyone. I just jumped on the bike and gave it a go. That feeling was incomparable, intense, and addictive.

As I improved my riding skills, I went with Marco on a ride to the city of Barquisimeto, in western Venezuela. This was a good five hour ride away, going through several major cities and National Parks. I was nervous and excited and left Caracas with the early light, soon realizing I also left behind the work problems, daily stressors, and the heavy aura of the capital city. Every kilometer was a conquest of effervescent testosterone, I was present and aware, and the ride made me feel light hearted, happier, and relaxed. We climbed the twisted rain forest roads of the Yacambú National Park and met Miguel Angel, a friend of Marco that lived down in the Tocuyo Valley, where we spent a couple days.

Miguel Angel Peraza is a talented ceramist, whose work has gained international recognition in Europe and the Americas. His house was built by his own hands. He molded and baked every single brick and fixed them to wood columns made from the railway ties of an abandoned train track. The ceiling in the living area had two large skylight windows, one on each opposite angle. One had an artisanal blue-tinted glass and the other had an orange tint. This was designed so the changes of chromatic hues would help keep the house at perfect temperature all day long as the sun rays traveled through these openings. The door knobs were vintage, ceramic insulators of old electric posts, and in the backyard, he had a vast miniature town sculpted in clay. I spent a great deal of time looking at the details and hidden stories in this miniature scene, while softly swinging on one of the hammocks he had all around the back porch.

I was fast to realize the people outside Caracas were different. They were responsive to milder vibes; they were kind, approachable, and communicative. The motorcycle was the catalyst element of engagement, a magnet for the curious, an open invitation for a chat, a gate to get to know new people. I felt connected more than ever and began to relate to these travel lessons and understand an old saying I had once heard, one that would shape my life in the years to come: "Life is about the places you've seen and the people you've met, everything else means shit."

I was enamored with motorcycles and long-distance riding. I had found a genuine, lifetime passion, and it became a personal quest to explore and to open myself to understand the world I lived in.

THE BIKE

THE IDIOT

From 2009, when I received my dual citizenship, up until 2016, I pushed forward with my plan to get to know all the fifty states of the United States. I couldn't imagine a better way to do it but on a motorcycle.

Without any trace of doubt, nothing was more fitting for this North American journey than a Harley-Davidson or an Indian motorcycle. I ended up buying a second-hand 2010 Harley-Davidson Dyna Street Bob, which I playfully named "La Loba," which is the Spanish word for female wolf. This name I found to play along nicely with "Motorwolf," the moniker I chose to identify myself on many of the social media platforms, and from that point on, it became a derivative nickname for which people started to recognize me.

You must be asking yourself what the hell is a Dyna Street Bob? Well, it's a 300-kilogram Harley-Davidson motorcycle with a rubber-mounted, large-displacement twin engine of 1584 cubic centimeters and a stripped-down design consisting of the bare minimum to be street legal. In other words, a pretty heavy motorcycle with no protection and no touring comfort features at all.

"That's just nuts!" you may say, but the Dyna Street Bob is the bike I fell in love with, and to be candid, it was the bike I could afford at that time. This bare and simple motorcycle was all I needed to start my plan of riding the entire country.

For the next few years, I made several cross-country rides on La Loba, covering many regions of America and checking several states off the list along the way.

In the early fall of 2012, I made my first ride for the fifty states goal. I left New York City and went north, riding across New England. I rode through New York during Labor Day weekend traffic, got stopped at gunpoint by a very young state trooper in Connecticut for splitting lanes, covered Rhode Island, Massachusetts, and spent some nights camping in the Acadia National Park in Maine. I kept going further north, crossing the Canadian border to hit New Brunswick, Nova Scotia, and ended up riding the Confederation Bridge all the way to Prince Edward Island. On my way back, I crossed through Quebec and Ontario, to later head south through Vermont and ride my bike up Mount Washington in New Hampshire before heading back home.

On the next ride, in 2013, I went from New York City to Los Angeles. This trip had a hidden agenda; I wanted not just to see the country, but also to go visit a woman from Los Angeles who I was crazy about back then. I crossed New Jersey, Pennsylvania, and visited the Rock and Roll Hall of Fame in Ohio, which at the time had a featured exhibit on the Rolling Stones. I rode Indiana, Michigan, Illinois, Wisconsin, Minnesota, Iowa, Nebraska, South Dakota, Wyoming, Idaho, Utah, Colorado, New Mexico, Arizona, Nevada, and California. This was an exhilarating ride, visiting many National Parks, and it was full of all kinds of stories, from riding in a police car in Chicago to confronting a buffalo on the road for the first time in Wyoming to having the bike blessed by the Lakota Sioux to visiting Yellowstone, Moab, and the Grand Canyon.

Early in the year, in 2014, by using the airline miles I had collected from several international trips I'd taken to visit my family, I was able to jump on a plane to Hawaii. I rode around Oahu on a rental Harley-Davidson Dyna Wide Glide, visited the surfer's mecca known as the Pipeline on the north shore, did some spectacular snorkeling in Hanauma Bay, visited Pearl Harbor, and stuffed my soul with delicious Hawaiian Lilikoi butter and purple taro bread, while sipping on macadamia infused coffee in the mornings.

Later on that same year, I ventured south, adding Delaware and Maryland. I visited the nation's capital in Washington DC, then rode to Virginia, West Virginia, Kentucky, and North Carolina. I visited Graceland, the iconic home of Elvis in Tennessee; then crossed Arkansas, Missouri, Kansas, Oklahoma, and turned back around in Texas, where things got really weird in Austin. Finally, I hit Louisiana, Mississippi, Alabama, Florida, Georgia, and South Carolina before I headed back to home in the Northeast.

The following year, I did the memorable "Astoria to Astoria" ride. Starting in Astoria, New York, and ending in Astoria, Oregon . . . any *Goonies* fans here? During that ride I added North Dakota, Montana, Washington, and Oregon to the list of ridden states; but also crossed pretty much all of Canada, covering Manitoba, Saskatchewan, Alberta, and British Columbia. The ride made me fall in love with the Canadian Rockies, which I considered to be one of the world's most beautiful motorcycle paradises.

After the knowledge and experience I gained on all these rides, I found myself staring at Alaska on the map and feeling intimidated. It was the last state left to be ridden on my list, yet there was something about it; Alaska felt remote, enigmatic, unpredictable, and wild, more than any other place I'd visited so far.

The truth is plain and simple; it takes a special breed of pendejo to try to ride all the way to the Arctic Circle on a bare motorcycle, without a windshield, no guard fairings, no saddlebags, and equipped only with street tires.

In the summer of 2016, I was that pendejo.

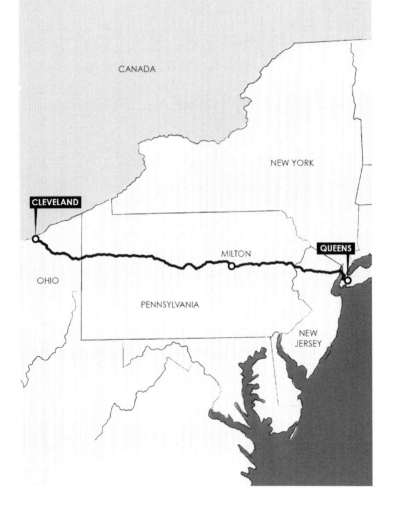

SECTION I

NEW YORK - NEW JERSEY
PENNSYLVANIA - OHIO

CANADA

NEW YORK

CLEVELAND

MILTON

QUEENS

OHIO

PENNSYLVANIA

NEW
JERSEY

THE FIRST LEG

It was a warm, summer morning. Megan was in the kitchen brewing a pot of coffee. She was still in her pajamas, looking soft and beautiful. I tried to imprint the image of that moment in my head in an effort to have a last minute memory of home for the road.

I realized all the abstractions of my Latino spirituality were kicking in hard. I checked that I was wearing my "colmillo de perro" necklace and a medallion I had made with a wolf head on one side of it and the archangel Saint Michael on the other. I packed a rosary I had gotten from my family and burned some palo santo to clear my path, while asking all of my dead people, "todos mis muertos," to show me the way. I'm not a religious person at all, but I also don't identify with nihilistic thinking. Being raised in a Catholic family made me find comfort in some of these imageries. The rest of my pre-ride rituals were a mixed bag of plain Latino paganism and a simple collection of objects that I bring with me that remind me of my kids, my woman, and my family.

The house filled with the familiar aroma of a Venezuelan café con leche. My mind was restless to begin my motorcycle journey. I went, once more, over the packing list and checked the bags. Megan handed me a mug and spoke with a formidable calm . . .

"Are you all set?"

"I guess. I checked everything off the list, and made it as compact as possible."

"I'm going to miss you."

"Me too . . . " I murmured, trying to hide my anxiety for taking off.

"Come back to me."

"Always . . . "

I felt the excitement rising in my body as I finished my coffee. I gave my Megan a kiss and a rather brief farewell. I strapped on my full-face helmet and pointed my motorcycle to the north, exhaling a deep "Here I go!"

I set my mind to ride from Queens in New York City all the way to the Arctic Circle in northern Alaska. This mysterious state was the only one I hadn't ridden in America, and I was determined to complete riding in all fifty states. My dream was to experience the phenomenon of the Aurora Borealis and ride as far north as I could. This ride I knew would be a monumental challenge, but I was ready to face it.

Long distance riding for me is similar to running a marathon, with a steady pace, rather than a race to reach a destination. So I decided to start with a short day in the saddle to warm up for what would be my next month or so on the road.

I left Queens that morning with a full tank on my trusty Harley-Davidson. I crossed the George Washington Bridge and cruised steadily across New Jersey on Interstate 80 for about four hours into the heart of Pennsylvania.

I figured that with La Loba it may take me a little bit longer to get to Alaska, compared to other motorcyclists riding those big bikes of the adventure segment like the Africa Twin, Ténérés, and BMW GS types, to name a few. Certainly, I'd have to maneuver slowly at times, but my thought was "If it has two wheels and an engine, I'll make it."

My first stop was at Steel Steeds, a fun and friendly motorcycle campground near Lewisburg, Pennsylvania. There, I set up camp right on the banks of the Susquehanna River. The campground was quiet, with only a few other people staying for the night. I pitched my old dome tent on a flat, grassy spot under a large oak tree, unloaded my bags from the bike, and swapped my riding boots for a pair of more comfortable slip-on sneakers. I sat in the open tent for a minute thinking, "¡Mierda! There's no going back now."

At a short walking distance was a conveniently located bar. The establishment was full of colorful country characters that afternoon, mostly bikers and truckers. I sat down at the corner of the bar and downed a couple of beers to burn some time. I watched people come and go and met a few locals. One of them, jokingly nicknamed "Chlamydia," was the heart of the bar, telling unbelievable stories of child support and the ins and outs of the county correctional facility. I knew right then this was meant to be a crazy ride.

Next day, I had an uneventful ride west, reaching the city of Cleveland, where I crashed at the house of Mikey Revolt, one cool and very talented motorcycle lifestyle photographer. Mikey and his wife, Kat, were at a wedding party that night, so when I arrived at their place, I pushed La Loba toward the back of the driveway, praying that I was at the right house. Well, at least I didn't I didn't hear any pissed-off dogs, nor see the end of a twelve-gauge barrel held by some psychopath neighbor sentinel aiming at my brown ass . . . and yelling, "Who the hell are you?"

I decided to walk into the back yard and smoked a cigar to celebrate my first miles on the trip. They had one of those garden hammocks hanging in the porch, and it was too much of a temptation, so I kicked off the boots and laid down, looking up to a beautiful starry night. Is that Cassiopeia? Hmm, wait, Orion . . . lights out. After what seemed like the passing of just a couple seconds, it turned out to be a good couple hour of snoring, I felt something shaking my foot . . . "Dude . . . dude, wake up!" the bearded silhouette of Mikey voiced. Huge smiles went off, and we chatted the night away talking motorcycles, art, and photography.

The next day, Mikey and I went out for a ride to a Greek breakfast place he raved about. Mikey took his beautiful shovelhead chopper and his camera . . . and soon the ride turned into an impromptu photo-shoot. As we rolled toward downtown, I was impressed with the skills of this man, standing up and laying down on his motorcycle, taking pictures and focusing with both hands on a full DSLR camera while in motion, giving the bike brief twists of the throttle to keep momentum and hoping for no jaywalkers to come across. I felt my photography skills were crushed in a span of three blocks.

At the Greek restaurant we ordered breakfast. I went for pancakes, and Mikey ordered some sort of Greek omelet. The motorcycle chatting was ongoing We shared road stories and talked about his involvement in the creation of Fuel Cleveland, one of the most important motorcycle events in the region. All of a sudden, I started noticing Mikey's face turning red. In my mind I was quickly trying to remember the illustrated poster I once saw about how to do the Heimlich Maneuver. Shit was getting real, and then he exclaimed:

"Man, you're going to kill me. This is a cash only place, and I forgot my wallet. I just have a credit card with me . . . so sorry, not sure what I was thinking."

"Wait, what?"

We had a good laugh, and I gladly paid the check . . . wink! Then we went off to finish the ride and take a few more pictures.

We cruised downtown Cleveland and stopped at the Rock and Roll Hall of Fame, the vibrant pyramidal building that shelters the history of the music that transformed my childhood. The sight of this place gave me a flashback memory to the day my older brother, Rafael, handed me a beige-colored TDK cassette and said "Here, listen to this". That was my very first mixtape. It had AC/DC, Rush, Kansas, Deep Purple, Jethro Tull, and a few Boston songs. I was blown away by this energetic music I'd never heard before. Almost immediately, I was obsessed with my cassette and the sound of these overdriven guitars.

On our way back to the house, I was riding behind Mikey. We turned to a major highway, when suddenly I saw a glaring object bouncing off the shovelhead. I sped up to signal him that something had fallen off his bike, realizing his entire shifting lever was gone. We got off on the next exit and kept going non-stop, otherwise we would be screwed, without a way to get the bike in gear. We cruised back to the same highway, making right turns at every red stop in order to keep moving. It literally felt like we were dogs doing circles before lying down, I laughed to myself. We got back somehow onto that same highway and slowed down to a crawl, as I kept my hazard lights on to signal the fast, oncoming traffic behind us. Suddenly, there it was! We found the damn lever in the middle of the highway. We pulled to the shoulder, and I took a set of pliers from my tool roll. Mikey wrenched the shifter back in place, while I was doing an over exaggerated monkey dance to make ourselves visible to the drivers coming our way. The lever was missing the actual toe peg, and all it had left was the arm, so Mikey ended up shifting his chopper back home by pressing his heel against the tip of the lever arm and "scooping" it up and down to engage gears . . . As I said, the man has skills!

We jumped back onto highway 77 to finally return to the house, and just when I thought all was falling back into a chill ride, a guy riding a souped up Harley-Davidson V-Rod zipped really fast by us. He passed so close I swear I spotted a picture of Jax Teller taped to his odometer, from his saggy pants, leather vest, and white sneakers combo look, I knew this was a case of a "Post-Sons-Of-Anarchy" biker. The guy slowed down in front of us and lined himself next to Mikey, turning his head and revving his V-Rod about a thousand times. I was riding slightly behind the scene and had to spit out a few feathers hitting me on the face. We just kept looking at him with our best Johnny Utah "Really, brah?" faces until he twisted his final dozen revvings and shot out into the horizon of C-town with his Hollywood-infused bravado. I never quite understood that kind of macho attitude some people acquire while riding, but hey, I guess to each their own.

After a short stay at Mikey and Kat's place, I left Ohio and thundered my way west on Interstate 90 with not much interest in the scenery. I stopped for a late lunch at one of the typical highway rest stops. There was a gas station and a cookie-cutter designed building filled with the usual chains of fast food establishments. I sat down to chew on a standard American road delicacy: a thin mysterious-meat burger and a few soggy fries served inside a cardboard box on top of a plastic tray cleaned with a mystery blue spray and an overused wet rag. It baffles me how first-world societies came to accept that as normal.

As I was eating, a cool young couple approached me about my vest, which displays a large Motorwolf logo on the back. While sitting there, they looked it up on the Internet and saw my travels, as well as my brand and line of motorcycle clothing. Sure enough, they were actually starting a new motorcycle clothing company called "Bad Grease." This somehow became another great encounter out of a routine "pouring ketchup on a flip flop" stop, and I ended up with a couple T-shirts and some stickers for free!

After that, I finally made it to Chicago, which is one of my favorite cities in the Midwest. This time I connected with Ken Carvajal through Instagram. The man is yet another talented motorcycle photographer I follow through that social media channel, and he kindly opened up his house for me to spend the night. I arrived late that afternoon. My delay was caused by the traffic I encountered on the Interstate, which was jammed with heavy-construction sites. Ken was kindly waiting for me, or at least I'd rather believe it was perfectly fine to show up super late at an unknown guy's house, with family life, and so on. Hey! But we both love motorcycles right, so cool right? . . . right?

When he opened up his garage, it was like divine light beams came out of it, with a few choppers and all sorts of motorcycle knickknacks loose around. I pushed La Loba inside while my mouth was foaming with saliva like a sloppy boxer dog. Damn man! What a sight. We had an easy night having a few drinks and also had the pleasure of trying some amazing South Asian soup. Ken is one of those people that, from the moment you meet him, you can connect on many levels—a soft spoken, remarkable photography artist that transmits a humble, beautiful light.

Ken set me up on a super comfy couch they have in the family room, where I rested for the night, surrounded by a collection of stunning motorcycle photographs on the walls.

The next morning, we went out for a quick ride in town, looking for spots to capture some images. We ended up in a small park in the Windy City's suburbia, taking pictures of the bikes.

Back at his place, we shared a few more riding stories and, recharged with his good vibes, I left for Milwaukee.

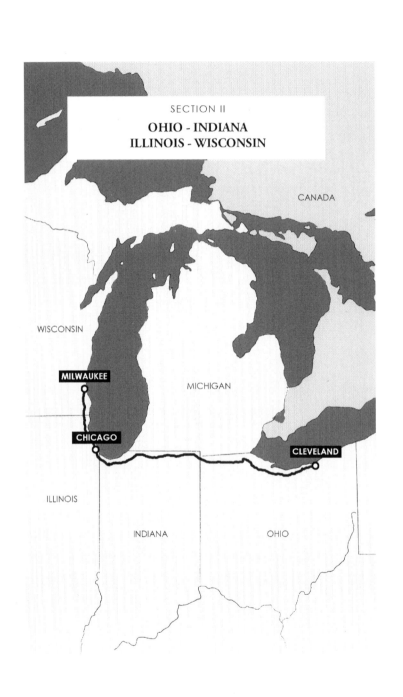

SECTION II

**OHIO - INDIANA
ILLINOIS - WISCONSIN**

CANADA

WISCONSIN

MILWAUKEE

MICHIGAN

CHICAGO

CLEVELAND

ILLINOIS

INDIANA

OHIO

HOGS AND PIGS

The ride from Chicago to Milwaukee is quite short, but the main highway is infested with tolls, for sure one of the most annoying things you have to deal with when you are on a motorcycle.

I was taking my time, since the trip was only a couple hours long, but I could feel my veins pumping through my arms after the fourth toll stop.

"There comes another toll, stay in line, Miguel, crawl slowly for the 'Cash Only' lane," since paying fifty dollars for the I-Pass is absurd. The guy in front was texting. Sigh, rev the bike to let him know he needs to move. Finally get to the booth, put the bike in neutral, can't find neutral, ask for the price, wait what? "I can't hear you! Wait, let me turn off the bike."

"It's eighty cents, sir."

Yelling in my head: "Are you fucking kidding me? All this for eighty cents!"

Reach for money. Damn, the gloves are now stuck in my pocket, "Wait ma'am, just a second." The car in the back beeps his horn once, I glance back in complete vexation and see a lady in a minivan filled with kids . . . "Relax, Miguel." Finally I grab a dollar bill out of my wallet. I get the change back and try to slide the coins into the pocket; a coin falls on the road. "Leave it!" The glove gets stuck again . . . "fuck!" Minivan beeps again . . .

"*Calm down lady!*"

I put the bike in gear and finally rode for just a few short miles to stop again and do it all over at the next toll! I cursed the crap out of I-94 and gave "mal de ojo" to everyone all the way to Wisconsin.

I arrived at Milwaukee later on that day and went straight to the Harley-Davidson Museum to pay the mandatory honors to this biker's holy ground.

I rolled into the parking lot, surprisingly not too congested with bikes as it usually is, and I noticed this one guy checking out my bike. He walked towards me as I was taking my helmet off and told me with a thick Eastern European accent that he loved the look of my bike and that he really, really . . . like *reaaaally* loved the Navajo saddle blanket I had over the seat. Immediately, my "growing up in a so-called third world country" senses turned on, and I decided to stay close to the bike until the guy disappeared. Well, that took a while, since he wanted me to take pictures of him riding his bike. I believe it was a rental Sportster. Anyway, I agreed in order to alleviate my suspicions. He went on his motorcycle and started riding toward me standing on the pegs, making hand signs to prepare for the picture. I thought, "Here comes the wheelie!" But nope . . . strangely, he just kept going around the parking lot standing on the pegs, until I realized that was it, nothing fancy, no wheelies, skids, or burnouts—just a good ole standing on the pegs action! So, I took one single picture of the Romanian man, and he took off with an inexplicable grin on his face.

I went inside the museum and took advantage of my HOG (Harley Owners Group) membership to check it out for free.

Hey! Insert angels chorus voices here. I think it's the only free thing I've ever got out of Harley-Davidson, and it felt like a small victory!

The museum has two levels displaying the impressive history and evolution of this iconic motorcycle company, a true statement of American ingenuity and its impact through the times. One can experience the evolution of their engines in an interactive room, see a comprehensive gallery of their bike models from 1903 to the present, and get inspired by a wall of gas tank designs.

My favorite part was to witness and understand the way Harley-Davidson influenced pop culture through generations; the statements made through fashion and modifications, the essence of our motorcycle custom culture. And of course, I couldn't resist sticking my face in the hole of a standing cardboard figure that made me look like Evel Knievel.

After they kicked me out of the museum, I literally had a guy walking behind going, "Museum closes in fifteen minutes . . . Museum closes in ten minutes . . . Museum closes . . . " Sigh! I took a quick walk to the side building to check out a special exhibit they had for the summer titled "Drag Racing: America's Fast Times." The show was a fascinating collection of cars, jackets, photos, stickers, and so many genuine historical testimonies of our cultural love for speed. Later, I went across the shop and grabbed a quick bite at the Harley-Davidson Motor Bar before heading out to try to get myself a motel room.

Milwaukee is usually one of those really chill cities where everything goes easy, except that afternoon. I stopped in at a few motels looking for a room without any luck, and I was told all the hotels were booked because the Wisconsin State Fair was happening in town. "¡No me jodan!" After many attempts, I was scooting around Miller Park on my way out of town, already hoping to find a city park or at least a Walmart parking lot in which to pitch my tent. I spotted one of those "Inn"-style hotels on Moorland Road and tried my luck. The place had a room, but it ended up costing me a little bit more than what my budget allowed. It was late, so I took it and figured I'll rebalance my numbers further down by camping and eating a couple cheap meals.

I had a fantastic rest in a plush bed and woke up somehow surrounded by my Glenfiddich flask half empty and an arid, dry mouth. I went down to take advantage of the complimentary breakfast, and as I walked around to check out the options, I noticed a sparky lady battling the waffle machine. I stood there half-asleep and cranky for a few minutes holding my styrofoam plate and waiting for my turn at the waffles. She was failing miserably at using the little hotel culinary wonder and finally asked me for help with a melodic twang in her voice. I guided her through the deep complexity of the two-step directions: pour the batter in the pan, then flip the handle, done.

She started the typical small talk. "Where are you from? What are you doing in town?" and so on. In our brief exchange, she mentioned her family was in Milwaukee for the State Fair. I realized I've never been to one of those, so I decided that was my plan for the morning.

I rolled into town and found a spot next to one of the main entrances to the fair. I parked next to the booth of an octogenarian security guy and asked him if he could put an "extra" eye on the bike. "Not a problem, son!" he shouted. I walked toward the gate, and the traffic was insane. They had a crossing guard whose modus operandi was to wait to form a group of people, before stopping the traffic and letting the group walk across, and of course, I was the first person to arrive, so I had to wait.

The Wisconsin morning sun was radiant, and the heat was brutal. I waited a little too long for comfort while sweat dripped down my butt crack. Finally, a group gathered and the crossing guard helped us pass. By the gate I saw an airport style sign with prohibited symbols of all these things you couldn't bring inside, one of them knives. I took a big breath and walked back to the lot to store my knives in La Loba, then walked back to the entrance, going again twice through the waiting of the crossing group. My blood pressure, I'm sure, was through the roof.

I walked into the State Fair and was amazed by the culture within it, with all sorts of stands and shows from all angles of life. From school camps to a Paleontologists club from bars with performing bands to all sorts of food, games, and cultural acts. Put it this way, they had stands with pizza cones and, wait for this, . . . mac and cheese bottom pizza! Say what! Forget about New York and Chicago battling for pizza; Wisconsin dropped the mic!

The heat was killing me, and I sat under a tree for a while, when a group of Native Americans took over a small stage near where I was and started performing one of their traditional dances. I was immediately drawn by the hypnotic drum beats and their costumes and enjoyed their performance while I cooled off. The native chants brought me back to the ceremony I had with the members of the Redrum Motorcycle Club before I left Queens. The Redrum is a Native American motorcycle club whose principles are based on the spreading of peace and good light. I've been a friend of a few members of the club for quite some time, and they gathered to give me and my bike a sendoff blessing. Sitting there and looking at these Native American dances made me reflect on the words I received that day. Cliff, the club president, who was also the master of the ceremony, spoke of the ancient links of man, nature, and the Great Spirit. He told me the importance of me connecting with Nature and reading its signs on my rides.

I realized for a second the heat was making me all deep and trippy, so I shook it off with a cold lemonade and walked curiously toward a huge building, where many well-dressed farmers were going. I'm talking men and women with fine white Stetson hats, tight Wranglers, and shiny belt buckles the size of mangos.

The inside of the building was divided into sections, each showcasing different types of farm animals. The smell was an unapologetic mixture of hay and shit, which I actually found refreshing, considering the peculiar stench of the subway platforms I had to deal with everyday back home in New York City.

I walked around, trying to understand the dynamics. The perimeter had all the caged animals and groomers, and then there was a main area, where some form of competition was in effect. I reckon they were showing goats as if this was the Westminster Show at Madison Square Garden. Owners were holding the goats and rubbing their bellies, while a long-faced judge dressed in a sharp tan suit walked around to point out a winner.

On my way out, a woman shouted, "Heeeey, you made it!" as I paused and recognized the voice, and there she was, the waffle lady from the hotel! She, her husband, and her two sons were there competing with two humongous pigs. They were very friendly, the people, not the pigs, and they explained the whole competition, which still left me scratching my head.

I stood there for about half an hour watching people steer their massive swine with long sticks. It's a frenetic thing; the pigs must be constantly moving. They made the pigs walk by slapping them with these sticks on both flanks, and that's all it was, just that, for half a fucking hour! I took pictures in complete awe and tried to make sense of who the hell was winning the competition and why? But I couldn't figure it out. The crowd on the stands was silent and super focused on the action. I could feel the tension, as if this was a penalty kick in the World Cup final. A judge made a final decision on one of these walking pigs. He pointed to the animal, announcing the winner, and people went ape shit. I looked around completely lost and thought maybe it was time for me to go back to the safe and familiar sight of my motorcycle.

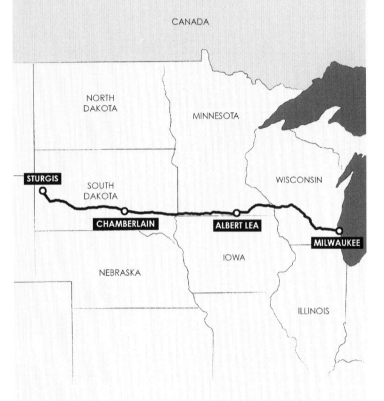

SECTION III

WISCONSIN - MINNESOTA
SOUTH DAKOTA

CANADA

NORTH
DAKOTA

MINNESOTA

WISCONSIN

STURGIS

SOUTH
DAKOTA

CHAMBERLAIN

ALBERT LEA

MILWAUKEE

IOWA

NEBRASKA

ILLINOIS

SIGN AT THE SIGN

AN ONGOING TRADITION

I left Milwaukee behind and continued my ride west. A few hours later, I was crossing the mighty Mississippi River at the border town of La Crosse. I stopped for a break at the Minnesota welcome center and took my usual picture, flipping the bird at the state sign.

Now I must make a pause here to explain this peculiar tradition of mine, giving the finger at the signs, since this has led to a few misinterpretations in the past.

It all started long ago, right before one of my first cross country rides. I was at a bar having a drink with a couple friends, and I was explaining my riding plans. They told me I was completely out of my mind to attempt traveling through all the fifty states of the American union on such a non-touring bike, with no windshield, a shallow seat, and no saddlebags. They pointed out that the idea was just plain stupid, and also dangerous. Of course, I didn't care for their comments and carried on with my plans, but I couldn't pass the chance at every state crossing to send my regards to the naysayers. And just like that, "giving the sign at the sign" became one of my travel signatures. I now have this very strange collection of photos of me flipping a bird next to almost every welcome sign in every city, state, and country I've visited around the world.

I've learned over the years that there is one fact every adventure and touring rider must deal with, and that is other people telling you how dangerous what you're about to do is. You will get bombarded with worse case scenarios and hyperbolic horror stories. But almost always, these concerns have been fabricated in the minds of people who have never even been to the place you are going to ride to.

Stereotypes are a stain in our society's consciousness, and they will come at you relentlessly, once you reveal your plans to others. You will be engulfed in plain cultural ignorance from people who have never travelled outside of their comfort zones and have spent their whole lives within a fifty mile radius. This inherent human fear for the ones that are different, the others, is a fact that, as a long-distance rider, and quite honestly, as a Latino immigrant, I had learned to deal with when discussing my next trip.

In my experience, people like this tend to not be genuinely concerned about you, rather they are partially jealous, sitting in their sedentary lives waiting for something to go wrong to quickly point at you and say, "I told you so!" And like Ursula K. Le Guin once said, "Nobody who says 'I told you so' has ever been, or will ever be, a hero."

Do me a favor, read that again with the voice of Morgan Freeman and throw some epic Hans Zimmer music in the background.

Now that I am in my forties, I feel that old renegade attitude from my teenager days resurfacing again, but this time not as the antagonistic prick, dressing in postmodern black in the middle of the Caribbean heat with an '80s mullet hairdo, and paraphrasing indecipherable lyrics from the Soda Stereo repertoire. No, this time my new-found, easy flowing, and careless attitude comes with a fantastic additive: experience.

Now I give full permission for life to happen, living in the moment with no conditions from others and not apologizing for that. I use my own flavor of common sense and try to go with it. Motorcycle traveling defines much of who I am and what I love, and I'm not going to stop experiencing it because of fear, so here is another big finger to all that.

Back on the road, I cruised under puffy clouds on the long stiff course of Interstate 90, with only a few stops for gas, to relieve myself, rehydrate, and to regain blood flow in my skinny baguette-like legs. Late in the afternoon, I made it to the town of Albert Lea, in southern Minnesota, and decided I had enough of farm views and crop dusters for the day, so I looked for a campground to spend the night.

The sunset over the flat landscapes of Albert Lea was magnificent. It seemed eternal and undemanding. The shadows of La Loba stretched long over the campsite fields, and the gleaming chrome on her engine flared into beautiful golden tones. The sun touched everything in those open spaces, creating a burning glow that made everything look soft. The warmth on my face and the gentle breeze were blessed gifts after a day in the saddle.

The next morning, I packed my stuff and left the camping site, heading over to the highway once again. I found myself crossing into South Dakota and stopping at the Valley Spring Welcome Center to give the finger at the sign and grab a snack. I felt the excitement of entering the American West and all it represents: huge open skies, mountains, and a wild sense of freedom that is so rare to find everywhere else in the country.

For the next three hours I fought the unpredictable and random wind gusts of South Dakota, at times making me ride literally at an angle, leaning against the wind to compensate for its unbalancing force on the bike.

As I got hit over and over by the wind, I felt like a birthday candle being blown by a two-year-old toddler, moving all over the place but somehow managing to stay on.

CLAY

SFMC

I arrived at the town of Chamberlain exhausted, with my shoulders feeling as if they were sprayed with a full bottle of starch. I went down to King Avenue and found a good deal for a small room at Lee's Motor Inn. I dismantled my bags from La Loba and went up to my room on the second floor to refresh myself a little. My epic battle against God's blow dryer left me with no energy, and I could have eaten an entire buffalo in that moment.

The lady at the front desk recommended that I go up the street to a place called Charlie's. She swore by how good their battered cod and cheeseburgers were. I rode my bike up and saw the unmistakable fifties-futuristic design of Charlie's sign. I parked alongside a few Harleys, realizing I was now entering the proximity of Sturgis, probably the most famous and biggest annual motorcycle rally in the world. Sturgis was happening the same week I was traveling through South Dakota, so it was definitely in my plans to stop for a couple days at the rally to enjoy the activities, not to mention the insanity of the party about which I'd heard so many stories.

I walked inside Charlie's and went straight to the bar, sitting on one of those red swivel chairs in front of a few TV monitors showing *Fox News* and *Monster Trucks*. I was surrounded by fishing photos and trucker hats. Also framed by my side was the quintessential Budweiser mirror sign and, behind the bar, a beautiful blonde girl, probably still in college, with the volatile character of nitroglycerine.

Sitting next to me was Scott Ian. I kid you not, the guy looked just like the metal icon from the band Anthrax, with one radical beard and an easygoing personality. He introduced himself as Clay. He was riding cross country as well and now was on his way back home to San Francisco. We sat there for a good couple hours sharing road stories and downing a few beers. Clay is one of those guys that makes one feel at ease right away, a calm paced "California dude" exuding good vibes. He showed me a few movies on his phone about his rides, and I realized he belonged to the San Francisco Motorcycle Club. This iconic club is the second oldest motorcycle club in the United States, being in continuous operation since 1904.

We had a good time and decided to share miles together all the way to Sturgis on the next day. We paid the grumpy blonde and left, and as we stepped outside, a massive storm moved in, throwing cats and dogs at us. I rode back to the motel as fast as I could, parking my bike under a covered hall, and finished the night watching the lighting spectacle in the skies, smoking a cigar, and drinking a Pepsi from the vending machine.

In the morning, we wiped dry our bikes and tied our luggage securely to the racks. Clay pulled out a striking helmet painted with the color scheme of the Irish flag, with two big clovers on the sides. I took that as a good omen for the road ahead, and it made me think of Megan, my beautiful

American-Irish girl back home. I must confess for a split second I felt "helmet envy" looking at my old plain Shoei lid, full of dings and scratches.

We rolled into town and went north on the picturesque Main Street to visit the Akta Lakota Museum. This Native American cultural center is housed in a modern building and has a comprehensive exhibit of the Lakota way of life.

Akta Lakota, which means "to honor the people", promotes the knowledge and understanding of the Sioux nation through the preservation of amazing historical artifacts and contemporary works of art. The place is magnificent and even includes many of the props used in the film *Dances with Wolves* as part of their collection on display. But my attention was fully grabbed by the Medicine Wheel Garden of Healing, an outdoor space that halted my in-motion reality and made me succumb to a peaceful state of contemplation. I closed my eyes and just breathed at the center of the wheel, feeling the warmth of the sun on my shoulders and asking with a quiet mind for protection on the road ahead.

After a brief meditation in the garden, I went back inside to regroup with Clay. We both decided to contribute to the place and bought a few gifts for our families. We also shared a "friendship feather," a simple, but nicely ornate, hawk feather that symbolized our bond as bikers and a celebration of the miles we would share that day.

We left Chamberlain with a fantastic view of the Missouri River, pausing to take a couple pictures of the road scene. Immediately, we stopped at Oacoma and filled up our gas tanks. The road was ours!

A comfortable, cloudy day framed the nice, smooth ride on the Interstate. We saw many bikers cruising in both directions, due to the rally at Sturgis being in progress. Clay and I took it very easy and cruised at just above the speed limit without any rush or concern. I thought, "This is what it's all about!" My mind was freed. I was floating ten inches above the ground living in nothing else but that moment.

After a few hundred miles and a handful of bugs had splattered in our smiling faces, we turned into Route 240 to ride the Badlands Loop Scenic Byway. From my previous cross-country ride around these lands, I knew how amazing this route was, but also knew that the Badlands marked the beginning of one of the most stunning regions in the country, covering South Dakota, Wyoming, and Montana. I couldn't wait to experience this one more time.

We rode slowly and easily through the many twists of the Badlands Loop, making many stops to admire the rugged formations in this strange geography. It was a spectacular view, and we kept putting our kickstands down to walk and photograph the beauty of the scenery.

First, we pulled into a sightseeing area that had an open view of this vast, tanned valley carved into hundreds of jagged canyons, creating a labyrinth of dry ravines where clay and dirt had eroded for thousands of years. I saw a "Beware of Rattlesnakes" sign by the side of the walkway, but that didn't stop Clay and me from jumping off the path and wandering through the terrain for a while. We hiked many polymorphic hills and played like kids under the South Dakota sun. Certainly, the spontaneous workout was a welcomed treat for our bodies.

It was midafternoon, and we stopped at the Cedar Pass Lodge to grab a bite. A friendly young woman of Lakota descent took our order and recommended the bison burger. I felt it was the most proper meal to order, being at the gates of the old West. The burger was terrible, but somehow the Marlboro man imprinted inside my head by the television ads of my childhood told me, "Shut up, Miguel, just keep chewing." It's funny to identify where some sources of absurdity and testosterone come from sometimes.

I went back to the bike, skipping the gift shop. I sat on La Loba for a moment, puffing on a Romeo y Julieta cigar, when another biker pulled next to me on an old yellow V-Max. We exchanged a few words, the usual destinations and road plans chit-chat, but his Yamaha brought me back to my days in Caracas, riding with my crew of buddies, tearing around the city on Yamaha V-Maxes, Maxims, and Viragos. I spaced out, and Clay tapped me on the shoulder ... "Shall we?"

We got back going on the swirling road at a good pace and stopped further down at another overlook lot. This time, I ventured a little farther off, looking for a chance to take a piss. I mean, all that desert-like weather had been keeping me on the water bottle. As I was about to unzip and take my chorizo out for a glorious relief, something moved in the bushes right in front of me. I froze and was ready to play dead like an opossum, then just like an angel, a young red-haired park ranger came out holding a pair of binoculars. I composed myself by holding a perfect Kegel exercise for my bladder. "Hi there, woman Ranger!"

We talked about her role in the park, and she explained how she was conducting an observation and count of the wild buffalos in that area. That was great news. I was already laughing at myself for thinking how embarrassing it would have been for my male ego to have a strange woman, in uniform, catching me urinating ... really? ... through a pair of binoculars?

As Clay and I cruised through the highest point of the Badlands Loop, we were forced to stop once more, but this time by a herd of bighorn sheep grazing on the side of the road. We rolled slowly with the cameras ready, when an imbecile in a Mini Cooper passed us accelerating abruptly, and making noise to put the herd on the run. I cursed his next seven generations, but at least I was able to snap a few pictures of the animals fleeing.

It was about four in the afternoon, and in the open view of the valley, I could clearly see a rain storm at full force coming in from the west. It was unavoidable; I was about to get wet. I pulled my obnoxious yellow rain gear from my top case and put it on, trying to get ahead of the storm. We gained speed on the last stretch of Route 240 that became a boring straight line all the way to the town of Wall.

I topped off my bike at an Exxon station in Wall and said goodbye to Clay, although he would be following behind all the way to Rapid City, where we would split. We headed back to the Interstate and rolled into a parade of motorcycles, as if the entire highway was owned by bikers. We got a couple of quick light showers on our way; the clouds were moving fast, so the rain gear was not really needed. I put my cellphone inside the waterproof pocket of my Lobo vest and carried on.

Clay flashed the blinkers of his Harley-Davidson Street Glide, and I waved him goodbye, as we took our separate ways. I clutched La Loba and gave her two completely unnecessary loud revs. Not sure why. I mean, Clay was not even in sight anymore. It felt good though.

SECTION IV

SOUTH DAKOTA - WYOMING
MONTANA

CANADA

WHITEFISH ST. MARY

MISSOULA

MONTANA

GARDINER SHERIDAN

SOUTH
DAKOTA

STURGIS

IDAHO

WYOMING

UTAH COLORADO

STURGIS

I pushed through Rapid City and made it to Sturgis. The town was on fire! Like a beating heart, the rally had its own pulse. It felt alive with the continuous rumbling of the bikes' engines. There were people everywhere, music, food, and motorcycles parked on both sides and the center lane of the main strip. There was a bike literally filling every possible open space. Locals even rented the front lawn of their houses for bikers to pitch their tents. And I'm sure good old Satanás sent the ladies a memo imposing a dress code of the barely necessary!

I found a spot right in front of the Harley-Davidson dealership on Sherman Street and sent a text to the good people of Kuryakyn, who I had previously arranged to meet at the rally. These guys kindly set my bike up before the trip with new LED turn signals and some motorcycle luggage and gave me the opportunity to collaborate as a friendly unofficial form of brand ambassador. I spoke to Serena, who worked at the time in the Kuryakyn product development department.

She said they were hanging out a couple blocks away at the Knuckle Saloon.

I turned onto Main Street and crawled with La Loba through a sea of people and bikes. A couple blocks down, as I approached the corner, a big guy started walking toward me with a camera as he was taking photos . . . damn! I felt for a split second like a rockstar and tried to look cool; you know, not making a big deal of it, doing my best album cover face. Then I realized that it was a familiar face. Talking about finding a needle in a haystack! "Keith!" I yelled. Keith is a fellow long-distance and touring rider I'd been following on Instagram. I'd enjoyed his travel postings and his sarcastic New England humor for years. So, there we met. It was super brief, since I had that meeting with the Kuryakyn crew, but was a sign that good people were around. I was so ready to party!

I parked right on the sidewalk over at the Knuckle Saloon, and Serena was there waiting with a bright welcoming smile. We walked up to the balcony on the second level, and she introduced me to two more guys from the Kuryakyn team. We chatted about my travels, some business ideas, collaborations, and the obsession of these two crazy dudes about doing wheelies everywhere, and with any bike they got their hands on. We decided get a table to eat, and on my way down, I got stopped by two voluptuous ladies who were hanging in the hall with their tits out, doing some acrobatics with their tongues . . . that sure made for a fun photo.

It was getting late, and after a basic bar meal, I split. I really needed to get going. I rented an AirBnB place I'd found in Spearfish, so I still had to ride for another twenty minutes or so to get there, and I'm not a fan of riding in the dark at all.

I had a text on my phone with directions to the place—one of those "Cross the railroad tracks, make a left at the second mailbox, then when you see a donkey, make a right" type of messages. I rode to Spearfish following a pack of bikes that were heading that way. I broke off the column to take my exit, and then the whole road turned pitch black, "Who the hell turned off the lights?" I was so glad I'd installed a new LED headlamp on La Loba a few months back, the "Daymaker," as they called it, really helped me navigate those roads. Further along I found Acorn Ridge, the road I needed to follow to the house. About a quarter-mile in, I thought, "Jesus, this is pretty wild out here." My thought was not even finished when two neon white dots popped in front of the bike. My mouth slanted in a perfect Stallone fashion as I yelled, "Deeeeer!" and applied pressure to both brakes, praying for no dirt patches. The doe jumped across the road, flashing her Bambi ass with a flick of her white tail, and I was lucky to swerve around the animal just in time. I composed myself and carried on at a ridiculously slow speed, until I finally reached the property gate.

The owners of the place warned me in our email exchanges that they had a pretty long gravel driveway to get to the house. What was not mentioned was that this road had a crazy thirty-five degree incline portion! Seriously? I had my legs out like training wheels trying to go down on the gravel slope. I carefully continued under a pitch-black sky. The trees around the trail made it so sketchy that some Spanish words inadvertently came out of my mouth along the lines of "What the fuck am I doing here?". At that moment I was positive this was the barrio of Petare in South Dakota and that was the road where people actually "disappeared." I believe it was close to ten at night before I managed to make my way to the house, finally.

The house was absolutely beautiful, sitting on top of a hill with a view of the Bear Butte mountain. It had a mix of modern style design with a warm country feel, which the wood construction and their tasteful western decor gave it.

A lady came to the front with a sweet welcoming smile. Her name was Talli. "I'm sorry I've gotten in so late," I mentioned. She told me not to worry and that they were up. She let me in and introduced me to her husband, Dal. They figured my accent out in a second pinpointing that I was Venezuelan.

Wow, now! That's impressive. Most people just glare at me when I tell them where I was born. And for some phonetic reason, every time I say I'm from Venezuela, people reply, 'Oh Minnesota!" Go figure. It turned out Talli had spent many years working in Latin America, and Dal was very much well-versed in the political situation of the region, being a veteran airman.

We let the night pass, engaged in an intense discussion about my experiences back in Venezuela. I lived through two military coup attempts in 1992 that forever changed the face of the peaceful and beautiful country where I grew up. I woke up to a state of chaos, with a scary martial law removing my constitutional guarantees as an individual. I woke up to an imposed curfew, tanks on the city streets, and soldiers shooting at each other in one of the most infamous fratricidal events in modern South American history.

My hosts were well-read and knew a lot about the Venezuelan situation. I think I was more fascinated by that than they were by my military uprising stories.

The next day, I woke up wrapped in quilted country sheets. My resemblance of a human burrito was a welcomed departure from my camping tent and the cheap motel beds.

It was an immaculate silent morning. I thought of my usual mornings in New York going to work to Times Square and had a giggle. Talli had made some fresh coffee and had some country bread at the table with berry jam. I loaded on the carbs thinking about my day ahead. I planned to ride down the Needles Highway.

Dal pulled out a paper map of the region and spread it over the table. I had a spike of testosterone and barfed out a totally inappropriate "Fuck yeah!". There was an awkward pause, then Dal continued pointing out good roads and places of interest. At the end, I made up my mind and decided to go for it all . . . "Fuck yeah!" I smiled and took off.

I rode back the spooky gravel driveway, but in broad daylight it seemed like a joke. I went back toward Sturgis and turned south on Vanocker Canyon Road. It was a perfect sunny morning to be out leaning on those smooth turns. I continued south on Nemo Road to Norris Peak Road to enjoy the Black Hills. The rain showed up a couple times in the more elevated areas, but I didn't care at all. The beauty of South Dakota was in full bloom, and I was on my bike, like a dog with his head out of the window in a car, with a grin from ear to ear. I took Route 44 west at Johnson Siding and merged south on 385 to stop at Pactola Lake for a brief rest. I wanted to take all this in through my eyes and connect with it all by composing a few photos.

Standing at the overlook, I was trying to take a mindless selfie with the lake behind me to send to Megan, when a short, long-haired biker with a ragged denim cut came up to me, "Hey man, do you want me to take your picture?" "Sure," I replied, giving the dude my cell phone. All of the sudden, the guy started a pushy fast talk and started asking too many questions. The hairs on my neck went up, and red flags were waving everywhere as the man kept talking and walking away further from me. He went on taking an unnecessary number of photos, so I did a sudden walk back to him and managed to get the phone back. He wasn't happy about my move, but there were a lot of other bikers at the overlook, so I guess that had to die there. He asked me where I was from, and I replied, letting my barrio accent run free, with an emphatic, "Queens, New York." I believe he felt the weight of the reputation of my borough coming from the words of a man twice his size, so he went back to his group.

Not far from there, I stopped at a place called The Country Store at the Forks to get something to eat, realizing I've been riding for a bit with not much in my belly. I filled up my gas tank and parked the bike next to the restaurant, taking my time and having a nice meal. I walked out with the intention to sit by the bike, smoke a cigar, and check out the several pop-up tents that were set up in the large parking lot, making business out of the rally week. But what I found was my bike surrounded by many other motorcycles parked so close I could barely swing my leg over her. I saw the same pushy guy from the Pactola Lake incident standing by the gas pump with his posse, and I knew this was completely intentional. At that point my best bet was to jump on La Loba and carefully maneuver around all that pack of engines. I felt it was safer to avoid any engagement with the "feather fluffer" and his group.

I managed to get myself and my bike out of that mess, like I was playing a game of classic "Operation," trying not to touch anything but my bike. I continued on Route 87, entering the famous Needles Highway in Custer State Park. Soon, a series of long granite formations appeared on the road ahead, gigantic columns standing up high since Precambrian times. I had to slow down for the spectacular view. It looked like they were the mountain's hands, with monolithic fingers sticking out of the ground. I rode hugging the hills and stopping several times to capture the scenery. It was a treat of sharp turns and exotic views for fourteen miles.

The road funneled down to a very narrow, one-way tunnel carved in the rocks. I pulled over to a parking area to check out the place, then decided to climb the hill and try to get a wider view of this natural wonder. I wanted to take a picture of one of the rocks nicknamed the "Needle's Eye," but after I took a good look at it from up there, I renamed it the "Needle's Totona," (one of the many Venezuelan slang for vagina, somewhat a "pussy" parallelism). I laughed hard at that, trying to figure how this obvious vertical granite vulva ended up being named as something else. I can imagine those park executives going in that meeting: "So . . . how are we naming this pussy?"

I took route 16A and did Wildlife Loop Road around Custer State Park. This road is supposed to expose people to some local fauna. Big signs at the entrance warn about not approaching the animals and list some precautionary measures. I rode for a while and saw a whole lot of nada. Leaning on a curve, I glimpsed a small whitetail grazing on the side of the road, then nothing else. "Too much hyped for a deer," I muttered, then I saw a bunch of cars stopped ahead and thought it must be something big over there, perhaps buffalos! I unmounted, with my camera in hand, only to realize they were checking out begging donkeys . . . burros for God sake! This started to look like the countryside of Venezuela, and I left shaking my head in despair for my expectations, and perhaps my luck.

After a disappointing experience at the Wildlife Loop, I circled back to Route 16A, stopping in the town of Custer, which was quite alive. It felt like a scaled down version of what was going on in Sturgis. I visited a trading post that had some Native American art, knives, vintage clothes, and several pieces of taxidermy. I sat outside on La Loba to smoke a cigar and got lost thinking that nothing in the store had any real value to me. I felt so liberated. I realized, once again, how much you can go on in life with so little. For sure, this is one of the biggest lessons that I've ever learned from traveling on a motorcycle. There's only so much I can carry on a bike, but it is as much as what life is going to ask me for. The feeling of being unattached to superfluous possessions is, for me, one of the true definitions of freedom. I ride; I'm free.

I headed north to visit the Crazy Horse Monument. I was there a few years ago on one of my first cross-country rides. That time, I met with some members of the Lakota people and had my bike and travels blessed. Their words were forever engraved in my mind and sparked my curiosity for the Native American way of life. After a quick view of the Crazy Horse Monument site, it is unavoidable not to think about the insane workload ahead to finish the largest mountain carving known to humankind. At the current pace, many generations ahead will not live to see it finished. We are talking about a statue that will stand 563 feet tall and 641 feet wide when completed. I walked inside their gift shop and got a patch commemorating Crazy Horse. I confess I'm a patch freak, and I collect these from places I visit as another way to document my rides. I also bought a pocket journal to keep notes for the rest of the journey. I love taking notes and putting down on paper the highlights of what I experience on the road, anything from writing down the names of places and people, to gas prices, small stories, directions, and so on. I found it is a good practice to always keep a pocket journal handy inside my vest.

It was getting late, and I thought I could do a final push to visit the Mount Rushmore National Memorial before heading back to the ranch at Spearfish. So, I twisted the throttle west on Route 244 and got there just in time to witness a spectacular sunset shining on the side of the iconic presidential sculptures. The sun hid behind the Black Hill's horizon, burning the skies with a bright red glow that lingered for long minutes. I was surrounded by numerous tourists from around the world, chatting and taking photos of the monument, yet for a moment, the place went silent in my ears, every single person went away. My mind made it all disappear, leaving me alone with the red glow on one side of the sky and a soft hue of fading blue on the other side, shaping the solemn faces of Washington and Jefferson and leaving the white granite carvings of Roosevelt and Lincoln ion a darker shade of Prussian Blue. I was in profound awe witnessing the colors of the United States flag being masterfully painted by mother nature over the mountains.

I was having my own patriotic moment, sitting on a cloud contemplating my own chromatic fascination, when reality struck. It was getting pretty dark up there, and I still had about another hour of riding!

My plan was to get out of the hills into Rapid City and take the Interstate to make it faster back to Sturgis. I came down from Mount Rushmore riding fast and crossed the colorful town of Keystone. Just as I was leaving the town, a couple young deer ran across the road and were a good reminder I was not riding on the FDR highway back in Manhattan, so I slowed down and decided to take it easy and play it extra cautiously.

I touched down in Rapid City after a sketchy ride coming down the Black Hill, on a twisty gloomy road with no proper illumination and nothing but hints of direction I got from the white lines marking the road. I was almost through town when a sudden downpour fell on me. I stopped in a parking lot of a Chinese restaurant, and by the time I pulled my rain gear on, it was definitely too late. I got a good soaking and there was nothing to do but stand there looking like the boiled wonton on the poster next to me. It was just how it is, just part of the biker life I'd chosen.

I waited for a few minutes, taking cover under the precarious restaurant awning. I cursed the skies for a while, and even chanted the mythical "San Isidro Labrador, quita el agua y pon el sol" rhyme that as kids we sang to stop the rain. Minutes later, I continued on my way back, zipping down the Interstate and braving the cold breeze of the night blowing on my wet clothes.

Back in Sturgis, I decided to stop and see what was happening before heading to the ranch. I took a walk around Main Street, looking at all the vendors and establishments and then ended up at Iron Horse Saloon. The place was jammed with people. I walked in just when a rock band was about to take the stage. I've never heard of them so had no idea what to expect, but the crowd was pretty fired up and the anticipation was intense. I felt the pressure cooker boiling, the increase in the crowd volume, the cheering and chanting for the musicians to come out. Man! people really wanted these guys. Then, a dude came out onto the stage with a flying-V guitar and threw a mean metal riff. He had wild long hair and theatrical face paint. I let out a "Hell yeah, they are going to Black Metal on me!" Out of a big puff of fog, two tall female figures appeared. They seemed to be in leather bikinis of some sort. I thought this may get kinky here. The crowd was hysterically screaming when finally, a woman appeared on stage center and started to sing. I was excited, expecting an act of the caliber of Gorgoroth, Immortal, or Watain, but all

I heard was something that I can only compare to the spooky themes of Scooby Doo. Well, that was it. I couldn't stand there for half a song. It felt to me like the music was a bit forced. Although it's most certain that I'm just getting old in my own ways, and perhaps my Metal standards are still stuck in the days of Ozzy, Saxon, and Iron Maiden. So, I went back and chilled by the famous Broken Spoke Saloon, ordered myself a beer, and killed some time watching the crowd of half-naked ladies everywhere.

I was spent from all the riding done that day, so I had a quick bite at a taco truck and rode back to Spearfish, once again, in a pitch-black night. I found the path to my AirBnB, although the road didn't seem so sketchy this time. As I rode down the smooth rolling hills, I realized the entire sky was sparkling with hundreds of stars. On a wide turn, I decided to stop briefly and turned off the lights completely. What a beautiful and peaceful spectacle that was, with none of civilization's lights around, in the middle of nowhere, alone under a veil of glitter.

The next morning, I said goodbye to my fantastic hosts in South Dakota. Meeting and sharing with Talli, Dal, and their dog, Marcello, was a refreshing time on the trip. We grouped for a photo, and I went on my way.

DEVILS AND GOATS

Later that morning, I crossed into Wyoming and stopped at the welcome center near the town of Sundance. I wanted to grab one of their free state road maps. Oh yeah, that sexy little sheet of paper! I unfolded it in the same lusty manner I used to let the centerfolds drop from a classic *Penthouse* magazine when I was a teenager. Looking at all those curves, man I sure got excited while looking at my route options. Weird shit aside, I decided my next route marker would be Devil's Tower.

I gave the finger to the state sign and made my way to this popular point of interest in the state of the cowboy, and the bucking bronco.

A short ride on Route 14 brought me up to what, at first sight, in the distance, my mind could only associate with a nipple, a giant nipple. Sure, I'd been on the road for a while, so don't blame me for my thoughts.

I got to the parking lot of this dramatic mountain and had to sit there for a while figuring out what my eyes were seeing. Devil's Tower is a drastically shaped mountain that elevates for about 386 meters out of nowhere. The side walls have a pattern of grooves that resemble a giant old candle with all the layers of wax dripping all around. Some say the monument is what was left from a volcano. I say this thing was a landing spot for extraterrestrials. Ask Steven Spielberg about that; he'll back me up.

I stood at the base contemplating in admiration a few defiant climbers. Looking like tiny color pixels on an eighty-inch plasma screen, they were already halfway to the summit, clinging to the vertical wall. I couldn't conceive the idea of being that high holding onto just a couple ropes.

I left Devil's Tower humming the mnemonic five notes of *Close Encounters of the Third Kind*. I rolled back to Route 24 and stopped not far down the road at a place called Devil's Tower View. The giant nipple was still lurking on the horizon, so the name choice for this establishment was pretty obvious. A bright red sign outside of it said, "Cold Beer," and I was pretty fine with that. The August heat was oppresive, and downing a cold cerveza with my meal was the proper lunch. I went for the no frills cheeseburger, which came with some tater tots, and ended up having a Pepsi, oh well. I topped the whole thing off with a delicious homemade strawberry rhubarb pie and a cup of coffee to kick it back on the road. That afternoon, I made my way to the town of Sheridan while chasing an unforgettable sunset on the clearest sky of the entire trip by far. The sun rays pierced me through the visor, and everything around me was slowly soaked in hues of gold.

I woke up early the next morning, knowing it would be a long and exciting day of riding. I wanted to go across the Bighorn National Forest, get to the town of Red Lodge and come back south to cross Beartooth Pass, then ride Yellowstone and get back into Gardiner, or possibly Bozeman, in Montana.

I saddled up and took Route 14 toward Bighorn National Forest. Riding up those mountains was quite a trip. It was a beautiful gradual climb with a constant open view of the valley below. This road lets you appreciate the magnitude of these lands with an unobstructed view, the same view the conquerors of the Old West witnessed from the back of their horses, a vast land once ruled by the Sioux nation, a land where their Great Spirit still lives in everything visible.

Devils Tower
Close encounter of the "third world" kind

I thought of the way the First Nations lived in those lands for many generations, evolving from endogenous and observational belief passed down from the elders, uncorrupted, untouched, with a cleaner state of mind, undistracted from being present and in deep communion with nature. It was unavoidable to compare their ways of life to our modern society, numbed on information and overdosed from the materialistic needle still hanging from its arm.

I stopped a few times along the way to enjoy the view. At the top of the mountains the road levels out at Burgess Junction, and I'd gotten to a place called "Bear Lodge," where I dismounted for breakfast. It was a cozy mountain resort that advertised the best omelets in Wyoming. I ordered pancakes.

After a great meal, a guy from the kitchen approached me and asked if I played in a metal band. I believe this assumption was due to my three days without a shower, my black leather full of bugs dress code, and perhaps my tangled, all over the place, long hair.

He went on talking about some black metal bands, and just to see where the conversation led, I pulled a bunch of band names from my playlist off the sleeve: "Sure, man, I love Watain, Gorgoroth, and Black Anvil. Not to forget the tasteful progressive black metal of Opeth, and of course, I hail to the classics like Iron Maiden." His pupils expanded like a coffee spill on a thin napkin, and he told me all about his love for those dark music genres. He also complained that living there was very difficult for a metal lover, having to travel for about two and a half hours each way to Billings, in Montana, which was the closest city that could, from time to time, have a metal show.

This was a relevant moment for me, realizing how coming from an extremely busy city myself, where everything is handy and everything happens, I was craving all this lifestyle, simpler and closer to nature. And on the flipside, this dude was desperate to get the hell out of it and move to the madness of urban living. We are only human, full of complex desires, contrasts, and imperfections.

I finished my breakfast by ordering a homemade cinnamon roll to tame my sweet tooth. I was excited for the typical pastry that we are all familiar with from places like Cinnabon and such, but then the waiter showed up with a tray holding a cake the size of a vinyl record. Yeah, I'm talking "The Cars greatest hits long play" big, swimming in a pool of icing and condensed milk. Just by looking at it I heard my stomach going… "Don't you mess with me, mother fucker! I'll rough you up later." Yeah, my stomach has a gnarly Queens attitude. I knew it would bring uncomfortable consequences, rushing for many "emergency" stops on the road ahead, so I had a couple bites at the "LP," about the size of "just what I needed," and got back on the road.

The last time I'd crossed those mountains I took Route 14 toward Cody to check out the rodeo, so this time I came down through Route 14A to make my way to Lovell and head up into Montana. I took a nice scenic ride that brought me to Red Lodge, hugging the edge of the mountains, which by then had me surrounded. Pine trees of colossal heights framed both sides of the pristine mountain road that would soon have me kissing the clouds.

I started a steady climb up the famous Beartooth Highway, a spectacular road that reaches an elevation of 3,337 meters. The views of snowy peaks and the many switchbacks made the road a true motorcycle heaven. No wonder it was labeled "The most beautiful road in America."

Because of the high altitudes, snowstorms can occur even in the middle of the summer, and the pass is also known for strong winds and severe thunderstorms. So, I took my time going up. I learned quickly that this mountain was no joke. I reached a serious altitude a bit too fast and immediately felt the lack of oxygen. "¡Mierda!" I soon started breathing in a fast, shallow pattern. I made a few ten-minute stops along the climb for my body to adjust and to take in all the glorious views.

I was able to spot a family of mountain goats balancing on the daring terrain. I was surprised to see firsthand how these stocky looking animals can move through the smallest rocky paths, stand obliviously chewing grass on the edge of insanely high cliffs, and jump from a tiny rock to another with the grace of a ballerina.

I reached the summit without any issues. I parked La Loba next to the sign that states the altitude, and for a while I sat on a boulder, staring at the range of mountains as they faded into the slate-gray haze of the horizon. Under my feet the deep blue Gardner Lake decorated the bottom of the vast valley. I let the minutes pass, with no care for time or destination, feeling the cold air tingle the blood vessels inside my nose, while hearing a Horned Lark sing his alpine melodies next to me.

As I started my descent, I visited the "Top of the World" store, a small charming shop that sits all the way up there on the Beartooth Mountain Range. I bought a souvenir patch and a small coffee and sat outside to drink my cup of dirty water with powdered creamer and a carcinogenic sweetener. Somehow, it tasted marvelous, or perhaps the views and my inner peace at the moment was just enough to feel grateful for something warm to sip.

A man, probably in his early fifties, stopped at the store on a brand-new Ducati Multistrada motorcycle, flashing its shiny Italian Red tank. The guy walked my way wearing the proper "Power Ranger" adventure biker attire. He asked me, in what I perceived as a condescending tone, how my ride was, as he looked down at my Dyna with an unmistakable judgmental smirk. I smiled and answered a laconic, "All good." He went on, uninvited, to spill his amazing travels from Denver all the way there, and the audacity of how he put those six hundred miles on that fine machine. I took another sip of my coffee. He kept going with his monologue, while unlatching his clean dual-sport boots. After a few minutes of his techy chitchat, I guessed he noticed the New York plates on La Loba. He paused, and with a diametrically opposite tone from the one before, he asked me if I'd ridden there from the Big Apple. I let go a, "Yep," he paused again. "So . . . where are you . . ." "Alaska," I interrupted, "I'm on my way to the Arctic Circle."

I walked to my bike not looking back, thinking this was probably how Clint Eastwood felt when he said his line "Go ahead, make my day." Man, sure, this was dumb, but it felt so good!

I rode down the Beartooth Mountain Range back into Wyoming, entering the northern edge of Yellowstone National Park through the town of Silver Springs, and stopped for a minute to look at the place where a few years back I had my first buffalo close encounter. It was a small cabin-style hotel where I spent one night then. I remember deciding to go out to eat, and what a surprise it was when I returned and opened the door of my room to find two humongous buffalos right on the front porch!

This time, I had plenty of daylight left to cruise the park, so I slowed down, knowing how active the wildlife is there. Sure enough, not far into the park, down Route 212, I came to a full halt due to buffalo traffic. There they were, about twenty of those massive bison laying on top of the road. I was right in front in a clear lane and stopped at a prudent distance to wait for the herd to move. I was probably about sixty to seventy meters away and had no choice but to put my kickstand down and turn off La Loba.

A few cars started to pull behind me, and the line became bigger by the minute. There were no signs at all of these oversized mammals having any intention of moving. I tried to observe their behavior and enjoy the moment amidst the buffalo. Laying down on the warm tarmac was "Fat Ass María," "Mad Cow Juana," and "Betty Beef" chatting about how their tits were destroyed by their calf. "Bill" and "Wild Wings" were chewing some fine grass. A youngster bull, known in the herd as "Soldier," was in the shady part of the road listening to some good old-school Reggae. Then there was "Sir Loin," with his square chin, a veteran, going around the herd collecting everyone and keeping it together. But my favorite was "Tommy T. Bone," a big dude, super chill, rolling in the dirt and making big puffs of dust, Tommy just didn't give a shit.

Buffalo traffic
Yellowstone Park - Wyoming

A mountain goat family
roaming the top of Beartooth Pass

The kid's imagination in me was having a blast, coming up with a full animated narrative of the scene, but suddenly that kid shit himself! Out of nowhere, a second herd came at my six o'clock and four humongous bulls walked right by me, so close I could see the ticks sucking their blood. I froze like the day my mom caught me, well wait, too much information . . . as I was saying, I froze and just let the beasts pass around me at their slow heavy pace, each of them larger than my motorcycle and three times its weight. I saw them walk ahead to join the rest of the group. Just then, a pickup truck coming in the opposite direction started honking and pushing through. Finally, they managed to clear the road from the animals. I probably sat there for a good twenty or thirty minutes, but the close experience, while stressful, was definitely worth it.

I cruised Yellowstone in perfect weather. It was a beautiful afternoon, with a nice cool summer breeze that followed me through the ride. I stopped a few times to photograph the scenery and the abundant fauna. I got beautiful pictures of not just bison, but also pronghorns, and those funny prairie dogs. From time to time, I paused my journey to rest my hand from holding the throttle for so long. I chose stopping at small creeks to wash my face or just to sit down and relax, close my eyes, and cool my feet in the moving waters, while spacing out to the sounds of the river. Taking breaks for short meditations is something I really enjoy, while I'm not, neither pretend to be, a spiritual guru or expert in the subject, I really like the feeling I get in places like these, being still, quieting my mind, surrounded by nature, and feeling connected.

After an amazing long day of riding, I ended up in Gardiner, back in Montana. The town welcomed me with a view of the Roosevelt Arch, a large gate made of stone that marks the northern entrance of Yellowstone National Park. At the top of the monument it reads: "For the Benefit and Enjoyment of the People."

It was already quite late in the day, so I went on to try to find a room somewhere in town. Because of Gardiner's proximity to the park, this small town was pretty booked with all sorts of tourists. After a few unsuccessful attempts to get a motel room, I was ready to give up. The room rates for the night were out of my budget, and the idea of riding at night time to press on to the next town was not something I wanted to do. Finally, at the last hotel I tried, I guess the lady at the desk noticed my frustration and made a call to a place called Jim Bridger Motor Court, a small motel that had a few wood cabins, and one was available!

I rode down to the Motor Court and it started to rain lightly. I saw a couple whitetails taking cover under the entrance of a bank right on the main road. I thought of New York for a moment, well, I figured deer going to the bank in Montana is not far from rats going to Wall Street. Seriously, this was clearly a sign I should have kept an eye on the wildlife that time of the night. I made it uneventfully to the motel and set myself up in the cozy place.

Later that night, I ventured into the heart of the town, looking for a good place to have dinner. I stopped at the Iron Horse Bar & Grille, which had a nice unpretentious feel, decorated with many antlers and old tin signs. The restaurant sat on the edge of the Yellowstone River, and the view while dining was just fantastic. I ordered the Bison Shepherd's Pie and a Miller Lite. That was one of the best meals I'd had on the ride so far. The ground meat tasted fresh and well-seasoned. I wondered how they were able to achieve that taste without adobo? But hey, the mash potatoes was buttery and had the perfect top crust. I went back to my motel one happy hombre!

My cabin had a nice porch with a wooden bench, where I sat for a while smoking a cigar and taking a few swigs off my flask. I numbed myself with the Glenfiddich while watching the rain fall. I had a great night of rest as the rain sang her lullaby—a soft continuous rumble of drops drumming on the gravel driveway and the sound of the trees shaking their leaves with the breeze. I looked up as the dimmed, forty-watt bulb inside the cabin slowly faded away, and I went deep as my body increasingly felt heavy under the country sheets.

In the morning I was a new man. I filled up La Loba with some premium gas and took off to continue on my way north. I was very excited to see more of Montana, and my expectations were very high after visiting Red Lodge and Gardiner. What I found for the next three hours were many small rolling hills tinted in a dead, golden grass tone, a very monochromatic ride that took me by the towns of Livingston, Bozeman, Butte, and Deer Lodge.

I wasn't really entertained by the scenery, so I pushed La Loba into a faster cruise mode, locking my speed around 120 kilometers per hour. On one stretch, I found myself alone on the big slab, with no sight of cherry tops. I gave La Loba a good twist of the throttle. The needle on the speedometer reached 145 kilometers per hour, and I felt free as fuck. I held tight onto the handlebars for a minute, taking the wind blast on my chest. Not having a windshield is brutal at those speeds, for sure. I was flying and had a madman laugh yelling something in the vein of "Me cagoooo en el arbolitoooo!" something that translate perhaps as "I shit on the Christmas Tree" as my cheeks wobbled with air. I quickly rolled down to my cruising speed with a smile on my face and a gratified sense of self-stupidity.

It wasn't until I reached the proximity of Missoula when the beauty of Montana reappeared, drawing mountain silhouettes on the horizon while I carved nice wide turns on the highway.

I rolled into the downtown area of Missoula and stopped at a coin laundromat named the Green Hanger. I was running low on clean shirts and sure my riding pants needed a good wash. I went to the restroom and took everything off and walked out in a pair of swimming trousers and a tank top. For the following hour and a half, I sat there going through the machine cycles and watching the spin of the soap bubbles through the round window lid. It felt like I was being hypnotized.

Missoula is a big college town, and my male imagination kicked in when an insanely beautiful brunette came into the Green Hanger. She walked toward a washer in the same aisle I was and began throwing her clothes inside the machine. She was young, in her mid-twenties, athletic looking, and with the abdomen of a Greek sculpture. It was hard not to look at her, and she caught me staring. I turned my eyes toward the ceiling but noticed her smiling at my clumsy move. In my head I heard a voice going, "You're an idiot." Then she started killing me with the daring seduction of a college girl. She would grab her undies and stretch them in front of her, like a doctor looking at an X-ray, before throwing it inside the machine with a giggle. I had a knot of thick saliva in my throat and coughed a couple times trying to clear it. Then she went on and took her shirt off. My jaw dropped involuntarily watching it all in super slow motion. I swear George Michael's "Careless Whisper" sax line started playing out of nowhere. A fine sports bra and yoga pants were the only thing standing between reality and porn. The fire in her hormonal years was enough to veto any inhibitions. She cat walked toward me, "I'm never gonna dance again, guilty feet have got no rhythm . . . ," more saxophone, hell is coming, so close, her eyes, she touched me . . . "Excuse me, sir, your washer machine time is up. You need to put your clothes in the dryer now. We're closing in an hour." I woke up with an embarrassing boner to the cranky voice of an old woman working the establishment. She was not amused.

The next day, I went around town looking for a good place to have breakfast. I asked a local for recommendations and he pointed me to the Uptown Diner on Higgins Avenue. The place, a classic all-American diner, had a colorful 1950s style. Neon signs, round swivel stools, booths, an old Rock-o-la, and half of an old Belair car encrusted in the wall was all part of the throwback decor. I sat at the counter and ordered my usual short stack of pancakes with bacon and eggs over easy, a cup of coffee, and a large orange juice. The waitress noticed my accent and asked me where I was from. I didn't want to go too deep into my migration history around this land, so I responded with a simple, "I'm a New Yorker." The guy in the kitchen heard me and, without hesitation, began to give me serious shit about the New York Yankees. I tried a few times to cut him off, but the guy was rapid fire, until I started to discern the inflections in his pronunciation. I heard him say "wicked piss" about a dozen times and blurb something about driving his "cah" through a rotary. "¡Mierda! A damn Red Sox fan!" I just bumped into a New Englander in Missoula. Honestly, I wish I had just said I'm Venezuelan and all I care about is fútbol.

I paid quickly, the Bostonian still barking baseball stats in the background. I found it funny, so I left him a healthy tip, but just to make the total of the bill twenty-seven dollars. I drew a gigantic number *27* and next to it the word *rings* and the iconic intertwined NY Yankees logo. For those not familiar with baseball history, twenty-seven is how many World Series were won by the New York team, while Boston has eight. I then instructed the waitress to show him the bill and to give my tip to that big mouthed cook.

Outside, I noticed my rear tire was running with thin tread and needed to be replaced. I called my good friend, Bill Koester, who I met in New York and who now manages one of the best Harley-Davidson shops in Illinois.

Back in Chicago, we met briefly for lunch, and he told me to call him if I needed anything up in Montana; that he knew people. Sure enough, in a matter of ten minutes, I received his call back. He told me to get to the Grizzly Harley-Davidson in Missoula and to ask for John in the service department, that all was set and they would get me on my way quickly.

That is one of the many things I love about the motorcycle community, how we help each other, sometimes even going out of our way to extend a hand to a fellow rider in need. The strong sense of brotherhood grows like an omniscient creed from the moment you start riding and sharing the road, the runs, the charities, and rallies with likeminded people.

I swung by Grizzly Harley-Davidson, and they had me back on the road in no time, with a new Scorcher tire in the back and also a few hundred dollars less in my pockets. I rode north on State Route 93 toward Kalispell, crossing the Flathead Reservation. The terrain changed gradually as I got closer to the broad waters of Flathead Lake. Many mountains rose up on the sides of my visor, and the road began to bend bordering the lake. It was a fun road for the motorcycle with a wide-open view under a sunny sky. I passed the towns of Dayton and Rollings and went up to Kalispell, where I stopped for some gas before making the final push into Whitefish, one of my favorite towns in Montana.

Whitefish is a charming town sitting on the skirts of Glacier National Park. As I walked around the town, I felt every storefront was inviting me to come inside—cozy tea places with old brick walls and wood columns, a couple beautiful stores that looked like barns, and many cafés and small restaurants with tables outside filled with happy customers. They all warmed my heart just by their charming vibe. I kept walking, then I saw this place, so beautiful and glorious, it brought a tear to my eyes and the brightest smile was drawn across my face. I ran with my open arms into this enchanting dive bar. Hey, don't judge me, I care more for a good bacon burger and a Guinness than a "caramel macchiato with almond milk, gluten free, low carb creme croissant" that cost me about double the amount of money.

I sat at the bar inside the "Bulldog Saloon" on Central Avenue. This friendly bar was decorated with hundreds of sport decals, team banners, and multi-shaped cutouts of sport celebrities on the walls. A big sign on top of the jukebox states, "This ain't no country club," an emphatic double-negative that was grammatically welcomed in my heart. I felt at home, and yes, I ordered my elk burger and my Guinness. After filling my soul with meat, bacon, and the Irish brew, I went to the men's room for a quick wash. I got a good chuckle at the decoration, above the urinals. It was a big photo collage of gorgeous naked women. So, I've got my well needed dose of tits and ass before continuing my journey.

I stayed in town for a couple hours, killing time before heading up to Glacier National Park. My intention was to hit the picturesque Going to the Sun Road at the golden hour to try to capture the vibes and colors of the sunset in the high mountains.

I rolled out of Whitefish with a full tank and went east on Highway 2. I did a mandatory stop at the town of Hungry Horse to indulge in one of the blessings of Montana. I'm talking about the sweet tart taste of Huckleberries. I paused at a "must visit" place called the Huckleberry Patch and loaded up on the magical purple berry. I'm a huge milkshake fan, so I went for it. One side of the place is set as a small restaurant where they serve homemade breakfast, burgers, hot dogs, huckleberry pies, and shakes. The other side is a nice gift store that has a wall of everything huckleberry. You name it; they have honey, jelly, preserves, syrup, chocolate, lip balms, waffle mix, pancake mix, ice cream, fudge, and more . . . all made with fresh local huckleberries.

The Huckleberry Patch has been there since 1949, and they are definitely an authority when it comes to this blue-purple gift of nature. The staff was also extremely friendly. I had an extended conversation about life and traveling with the lady behind the register as I bought a couple postcards to send home. Believe me, I didn't want to leave that place. I also have to confess that, from time to time, I go online and order their huckleberry syrup and have it shipped to my home in New York.

I continued into the gateway of West Glacier, passing the tourist place where a year ago I stopped and got convinced into getting an old-world picture of me in a cowboy costume. The echoes of my past "Astoria to Astoria" ride were pretty alive as I crushed kilometers around this part of the country. I started my climb up the Going to the Sun Road, this time from west to east, which would place me in the outer lane, or better said, the "drop" side of the road.

It was late afternoon, and the alpine breeze was gentle. I cruised for about fifteen kilometers on the silky road bordering Lake McDonald, the sun still shining on its waters, reflecting uncountable glares of light in my riding glasses. Tall blue spruce and pine trees spread their scents as the road started to get deep inside the mountain walls. I stopped several times to document the ride and to make my best effort to take it all in.

The road continued climbing, and I reached a steep hairpin turn called "The Loop." From that point on I had the afternoon sun on my back, with the perfect light showing me the way to the summit, stretching a long shadow in front of the motorcycle. The road narrowed as I gained altitude, leaving barely enough space for two cars to slowly pass each other. The almost vertical cliff by my side was growing steeper, and it was very nerve-racking to be riding a motorcycle only a couple meters from the edge. I had to stop for a couple minutes at some construction they had going at the "Triple Arches," a small medieval-looking stone bridge that holds the small road against the face of the mountain. The whole stretch of road, all the way to the summit, made me feel full of life, daring to cling to the thin line that scarred the face of these colossal mountains, veering by the edge of boundless valley views, sitting on a motorcycle, with my own set of wings, exposed, free.

Three magnificent sharp, snow covered peaks appeared in front of me, and nested in them was a wide turn on the road with a place to stop to check it out at an overlook. I took my camera and went for it. The view was infinite, and from there I could trace the thin line that defined the road I'd just crossed.

As I walked back to La Loba, I saw a male mountain goat walking toward the bike. "Are you kidding me? What business does this thing have with my motorcycle? What does he care about cubic displacement?" He stood there, looking at the bike, maybe smelling the dirty laundry from my luggage, hell, what do I know! One thing I was sure about, there was no chance in hell I was shooing the beast off. In any case, I kept my distance and waited for the large white goat to move away.

I arrived at Logan Pass, which sits at the summit of the Going to the Sun Road, at an elevation of little over 2,000 meters. I walked to the rangers station to refresh myself and then went for a little hike. I took a small trail that took me away from all the tourists and gave me an unobstructed view of Clements Mountain's peak. I kicked my boots off and sat on the subalpine grass, crossing my legs and straightening my back bone. I closed my eyes and took a few deep breaths, filling my lungs with the crisp glacial air and letting it go slowly through my mouth. After only a few minutes I was connected, at ease with my surroundings, contemplating the creation of nature from the perspective of my minuscule existence. The sun was now resting behind the mountains, and its crepuscular rays shot perfect lines that contoured the snowy ridges. I had a moment of peace, humming in solitude prayers for my loved ones. A profound feeling of gratitude for life filled my soul.

In my meditation, I thanked my parents, in whatever dimension they are now, even if it's only in my head. I thanked them for encouraging me to live a life of adventure, to take risks, and for teaching me that true riches come from the heart and not from money. Now I was here, on top of North America's spinal cord, watching the sun exhale its last rays of the day.

I went back to the bike and started my descent toward Saint Mary. Somewhere I needed to find a place to camp before the night fell over me. I came to a sharp turn by the crossing of Lunch Creek, and as I cleared it, I saw a bighorn ram appear from the bushes over the ridge of the road. I stopped and moved slowly to pull out my camera and the long lens. The beast just stood there, immobile, proud, with its chest swollen and its looping horns high, like a statue from a financial institution of some sort. I finally clicked the shutter on the camera when things got pretty funky. The sonofabitch jumped onto the road. Now we were about fifteen to twenty meters apart. I took cover, kneeling behind the motorcycle, but kept taking pictures. The ram didn't take his eyes off me, it was a challenging look, and then turned full head-on toward

Challenged by this Bighorn Ram
making warning gestures he was about to charge my bike

Fortunately, he turned away, but not before he made sure
I knew who was the boss!

the motorcycle! I said out loud, "Mierda, I'm fucked! This thing is going to ram my bike; this trip is very much doomed!" For a split second, the air filled with a muted tension, like a duel in a western movie. I could hear his snored breathing. At this point, another younger male came out of the bushes, and the whole scene became very unsettling. Just in case, I put my bike's ignition on and had her ready to start, hoping to scare the animal with the pipe's noise. It got sketchy as fuck when the damn bighorn lowered his head toward me! I thought, "Shit! Here he comes . . ." but fortunately, a couple cars passed by right on time and stopped at the sight of the animals. I signaled them from behind my bike, in case I needed to run into their cars. But the rams, I suppose, got discouraged by the commotion of cars and people, so the alpha bighorn looked at me once more, knelt a little and took a massive piss on the road, before retreating down the hill. I'm sure this was his way of saying, "Take this asshole. These are my mountains. I rule here." I believe I, as well, peed myself a little.

I had a mixed feeling of relief seeing the bighorns go away and also for the accomplishment of capturing the close encounter with my camera. "That was one of those *NatGeo* moments of the trip, for sure," I chuckled.

I continued on my way down the Going to the Sun Road bordering Saint Mary Lake. The full moon emerged over the mountains in all her splendor, shining over the mutating color palette of the twilight. Orange and purple strokes covered the Montana skies above me while I heard the quiet whistling of the wind in my ears.

I paused at the sight of Wild Goose Island, one of the most photographed places in Glacier National Park. The tiny island stands in the middle of Lake Mary, surrounded by larger mountains. Wild Goose Island also plays a role in its own folktale. The legend says that long ago two native tribes lived on each side of the lake with no contact with each another. One day, a beautiful woman from one of the tribes swam out to the island. A handsome warrior from the other tribe noticed her and swam to the island to meet her. They instantly fell in love and got engaged. When they returned to their tribes, the elders demanded that the engagement be broken. The couple didn't agree with the chiefs and met at the island to escape and find their own land. The next day, the tribes sent war parties to get them back, but the Great Spirit heard their call of love and turned them into geese so they could fly away and be together forever. The warriors only found two geese rubbing their necks together on the island.

Wait a second, sorry amigos . . . So, I guess Great Spirit likes to play cruel jokes. I mean, think about it, turning people into geese. He could have drowned the warrior guys or given the couple a damn magical boat with a cooler filled with beer and a kickass stereo system so they could just scoot away, or in any case, turn them into something more glorified, like bald eagles. But no, they became geese. Think of the disappointing face of the lovers looking at themselves covered in feathers and shitting little pellets. Excuse the little iconoclast guy in my head, always getting amused with the surreal stories people come up with about their gods. The truth is all these folk tales are imprints of our cultural imagination that play an important role enriching our traditions.

There is abundance of myths in the Venezuelan folklore, like the horrifying cries of "La Llorona," the weeping woman. The legend says she fell in love with a soldier, who abandoned her after their baby was born. In an act of desperation, she killed the bo, and became insane after realizing what she did. She died of sadness and remorse. And now her cries are heard in the middle of the night, while she wanders around trying to snatch children. One can understand why parents tell this story to children when they don't want to go to bed early.

Even more sinister is the tale of "El Silbón," or "The Whistler." This was a young farmer man who had a beautiful girlfriend, but his father didn't approve of their love relationship and so he killed her. The young man then murdered his own father in revenge. After that, his grandfather punished him, tying the young farmer to a tree and beating him with a whip. The grandfather condemned the bleeding young man to forever carry a sack on his back with his father's remains inside. The old man also cursed the grandson as he walked away wounded "You will be damned for all of eternity!" According to the legend, the ghost of the young man can be heard at night in rural country roads as he whistles a chromatic scale of ascending notes. This is his warning, as he brings death or misery to anyone who comes across his path.

Well, I guess becoming a goose is not as bad, after all, certainly better than being snatched by a maniac woman or being murdered by a Venezuelan farmer carrying a corpse on his back.

Earlier that night, I made it down to Saint Mary, blessed with the bright light of the full moon. I set my tent on a campground at the base of Glacier National Park and rested for the night, still with the images of that day's rides in my mind.

A cupola of stars covered the sky. I laid outside my tent contemplating the minuscule window of the universe I was given that night. I followed my finger drawing constellations in the sky: Orion, Cassiopeia, Ursa Major among my favorites. I travelled back to the Boy Scout days of my youth, where I learned of astronomical concepts and survivalist orientation in the outdoors.

The moonlight waved at me on and off through the thin cover of my tent. I took a couple swigs from my flask, wrote a few notes in my journal, and surrendered to the warmth of the sleeping bag.

SECTION V

**MONTANA - ALBERTA
CANADA**

BANFF

CALGARY

BRITISH
COLUMBIA

ALBERTA

CANADA

USA

ST. MARY

MONTANA

OH CANADA!

GOD WORKS AT TIM HORTONS

The next morning, I filled the tank and went for breakfast at a small café right on the intersection where the Going to the Sun Road ends at Highway 89. I talked for a bit with a man that showed up on an old white shovelhead motorcycle. The distinct sound of that engine was a dude magnet. As soon as he pulled over at the café, many guys approached him to check out the vintage machine.

That day I was planning to cross into Canada, so I double-checked my documents and also packed my knives along with my camping gear, instead of carrying them with me. I packed another one of my knives in the tool roll as well to avoid any inconveniences at the border. After breakfast, I went nonstop to the US/Canada border crossing at Carway.

The border had very light traffic that morning, and I got my inspection almost right away. I went through the routine questionnaire of the border patrol, but this time they let me in without any issues. I must say, in all my years of riding in North America, I've learned the fact that going into Canada, for the most part, is a very friendly experience, quite the opposite of coming back into the United States, where the border patrol gets stricter and intimidating and, at times, plain rude, even to their own citizens . . . at least in my own experience.

This time the Canadian officer just needed to know how many days I was planning to stay in Canada and if I had enough money to sustain my trip. After the quick formalities, I was on my way. I did my mandatory quick stop at the Alberta welcome sign and flipped the bird for the camera.

Hello Canada! Goodbye cellphone signal!

I rode north on Alberta's Highway 2, very much happy to adjust my speed from miles to kilometers, and fighting the cross winds of the Canadian open farm lands. Without a doubt, my first stop was at the first Tim Hortons I found. Those places remind me of Dunkin Donuts, and you all know how we North Easterners worship Dunkin!

Tim Hortons had been a great place for me to connect to free Wi-Fi on my previous travels across Canada. Plus, their turkey sandwich had saved me a few times. They're a perfect quick and cheap lunch on the road. I bought a small coffee and sat down to send a text to my good friend Stefani, known by many as "Slickpepper." We had planned to meet later that day in Banff to ride together for a couple days.

The truth is there's not much to see in that southern part of Alberta, so I pressed ahead for a couple hours, making a halt at the Bomber Command Museum of Canada in the town of Nanton.

The museum is tucked off the main road, a true gem I was glad to find along my path. At the entrance there is a solemn statue of a soldier dressed in uniform from the Great War, holding a carbine with its barrel resting down on the ground. A plate honors the Canadian soldiers from Nanton who served in both the First and Second World War. There's also a wall with the names of the ones who serve on the Bomber Command. Inside there's a series of rooms displaying everything from paintings, artifacts from the war, uniforms, letters, and plane models. The visit finished in a large hangar with many actual bomber planes from different eras.

Their collection of aircraft includes a great looking German Messerschmitt 109. Those planes were the "backbone" of the Luftwaffe during World War II, and until today are the most produced fighter aircraft in history, with 35,000 units built. They also have a few Lancaster Bombers, one of the most famous and successful heavy bombers of the war. It became the central aircraft for the many night time bombing missions of the British RAF and the Royal Canadian Air Force.

As a creative director with a background in illustration and graphic design, my full attention was devoted to their large display of "nose art." The paintings of beautiful pinup girls and Sunday paper cartoon characters made the pilots and crew members of each plane feel closer to home. They proudly displayed their insignia on the nose of their aircraft and on the back of their bomber jackets. The bravery, humor, and irreverence in those paintings evoked a sense of comfort and belonging; symbols that amalgamated a few men with a particular machine who faced uncertainty. This visual concept resonated in me, as I dance close to a culture of motorcycle and riding clubs, where brotherhoods are formed many times around patches, colors, and machines. The biggest lesson of this unanticipated museum visit was to realize we are all fighters, surviving one way or another.

I bought a couple patches of the RCAF in the museum gift shop, and continued on my ride toward Calgary. I made it quickly to the city and tried to skip the urban traffic but got caught in the peak of the rush hour, and after a few turns, I ended up getting lost in the city grid. With no signal on my phone and no GPS, I had no other option but to stop and ask people for directions. This is something I do many times on purpose, as an excuse to connect with the locals and see what happens. This time, a fellow biker on another Harley-Davidson Street Bob, just like mine, same color and all, went out of his way to lead me to the edge of town and put me on the Trans-Canada highway that would take me straight into Banff.

I rode up to the Canadian Rockies under a very light rain. It wasn't enough to make me stop and put on the rain gear, but for sure, was enough to bring the temperature drastically down. Canada has a morbid way of finding your bones and shaking 'em.

The smooth Canada Highway 1 led me slowly alongside the Bow River Valley to the town of Canmore, where I grabbed a quick snack and filled the gas tank. About half an hour later I was entering the picturesque mountain town of Banff. I couldn't believe I was there just a year before, falling in love with this manicured town and promising that I would come back someday. I never thought it would happen just one summer later.

Because of all my delays in Calgary, Stefani and I decided to meet at Storm Mountain, where we had cabins booked for the night. I arrived with the last light and was greeted by my good friend right by the offices of the lodge.

"Slickpepper" Stefani is an all-around country woman, fun, sweet, and a firecracker when it comes to her beliefs and opinions. She is a fierce lady in everything she does. She knows her way around tractors, Jeeps, horses, farm work, and is probably one of the best female motorcycle riders I know. She rides an impressive Harley Softail with killer ape hangers and handles it with such grace that it makes it look like she's riding a bicycle. She's also the best local guide I could ask for to ride around the Rockies. On the ride I did from Astoria to Astoria the previous year, Stefani showed me part of Banff and gave me the local tour. I was thrilled to ride with her again.

We sat down at the Storm Mountain restaurant and I ordered the elk carpaccio and a bison tenderloin. I wanted to treat myself to a proper meal, something typical from the local cuisine. We chatted for a while, catching up with life, and had the mandatory motorcycle stories exchange, talking about travels,

Banff National Park
Canada's Motorcycle Heaven

places, and routes. We talked about our bikes' new modifications
and the ups and downs of our motorcycle lifestyles.

That night I had a glorious rest. The log cabin had a wood
burning fireplace and an antique clawfoot tub. The wall was

adorned with paintings of mountaineer motifs and a pair of old teardrop snowshoes with rawhide laces. I dropped all my bags and hung my helmet on a forged iron hook on the wall. I took a long hot shower, and later, I disappeared under the quilted covers decorated with tan and green printed bears and wolves. On the ceiling, a chandelier made of antlers dimly shed its light over me. I went easily into dreamland with the smell of old wood and my sweaty socks, probably the reason I took full cover under the sheets.

In the morning, Stefani and I rode down to Banff for a visit and to take a nice walk around town. We visited the Park Canada Building that sits on a hill at the end of Banff Avenue. The old stone building was surrounded by Cascade Gardens, a beautiful open space with stone paths leading to gazebos and with all sorts of multicolored flowers. We spent a good part of the morning walking in the downtown area, checking out the vintage and mountain stores. I stopped at the post office to send a couple postcards back home, and later we sat for lunch at the Maple Leaf, a nice restaurant tucked in a corner of Caribou Street. All in all, it was a nice easy morning, but it was time to make our way to Jasper.

Lake Louise was a priority on my list of places to visit that day. I was eager to experience the sacred glacial place one more time. As we approached the road to the lake, I had a rush in my head of all the memories from the year before. With every inch my grin grew wider, and I felt an exhilarating pulse in my chest.

I rode by and glanced at the cozy Paradise Cabins and the flashy Deer Lodge, all now familiar to me. At Lake Louise, the parking lot was full at that time of the day, packed with tourist buses and cars, but the park rangers conveniently set a corner aside to accommodate only motorbikes.

We walked toward Fairmont Chateau, the hotel building by the lake. We were escorted by the intonations of a mockingbird, the smell of fir, and the constant hum of the tourist crowd, stopping every few steps to wait for two Asian teen girls in front of us to pull out the selfie stick and snap a picture with their tongues out and doing the peace sign.

Lake Louise
Banff

I sat to contemplate the scenery on a large rock by the lake shore. In an instant, I was in synchronicity with the tranquil waters, breathing to the soft pulse of its energy. The sound of the crowd went completely mute, and all I felt was the irradiating glimmers of the light exciting my retinas and the crisp flow of air passing through my lungs. I succumbed to the peaceful ways of the turquoise mirror lake, reflecting the colossal mountains that surrounded me, standing like titans wearing the coats of ancient ice on their shoulders, like timeless vigilantes of a world so distant, a world we can only speculate about, a world before all of us, all of this, all of now. I was fascinated with the thoughts of prehistoric creatures roaming these lands and imagined the sense of awe of the first men that ever looked at this place, being just the same as mine. My euphoria reached the highest level I've ever felt. I couldn't resist taking a selfie doing the tongue-out-peace-sign thing.

After a failed attempt to hike to one of the nearby hills, we got back to the bikes and continued on our journey. Suddenly, a funny feeling in my stomach kicked in, and this was not the happy butterflies kind, but the gnarly stinging hornets. I disregarded the brief discomfort and kept on with the ride.

We hit the road to Moraine Lake, going swiftly through a stretch framed by white sharp peaks. The lake is vast and serene, resting at the foot of the Rockies, edged by a ring of tall pines of all sorts. We walked around the lakeshore taking pictures and enjoying the breathtaking views. I told Stefani I needed to have a moment for myself to do a little meditation. I walked up a hill on a partially covered trail, and after a few yards, I found myself following a small creek running on a bed of moss of an impossible green. The silence was now only interrupted by the low frequency undertones of the water streaming, running down over pebbles. I was thankful for such a meditative moment. Lake Moraine is by far one of the most picturesque places I've seen, where I felt utterly connected with Mother Nature.

The road to Jasper was pristine, the black tar was smooth and fast. La Loba felt as if she hovered a foot or so above the ground, awakening flashbacks of my childhood. I was a fighter pilot, flying my P-40 Mustang, shooting down a dozen Stukas; I was Skywalker swerving frantically through the cracks of the death star; I was El Zorro, well there's not much analogy there, but El Zorro is the coolest dude . . . so that's that.

Halfway to Jasper, the afternoon dimmed on us. Stefanie knew of a hotel at the Saskatchewan River Crossing, and we decided to share the cost for a double room. I was hoping to reach Jasper that day, but my stomach was still feeling weak, and I thought it was wise to not push my body.

I woke up the next morning somewhat apologetic, self-conscious of my loud, bear-like snoring. Stefani was kind to not bring it up, but she hinted she had a restless night. I blushed and started packing my bags, quickly mumbling, "I'll be outside checking the tire pressure on the bikes," just to avoid elaborating on the topic. My luggage mounting routine is very fast. I chose my bags and designed a system so I could easily pack and unpack the bike in under five minutes. I don't like to dwell on these routine tasks and would rather use that time on the road. That said, I waited for Slickpepper, and twenty-three minutes later, we were both on our bikes.

As we were about to leave, Stefani's bike made a clicking sound at the touch of the electric starter. A few tries resulted in the same Trrrrth! Trrrrth! Fuck! The battery was dead.

After all the complex tying of bungee cords she did to pack her bags, it all needed to come off the bike again. I pulled my tool roll, while Stef removed the bags and the seat off her Softail. While this was happening, a coach bus packed with Chinese tourists stopped nearby on the lot, then it felt like a paparazzi moment. None of them spoke any English, but I heard a couple "Haley Déiviso" here and there. The hotel maintenance guy came to the scene and lent us a battery crank, but it didn't work. Stefani was clearly feeling upset, so I tried to keep a positive angle on the mishap. She decided to go for a walk to regroup herself, and I waited by the bike. The Chinese crowd grew bigger. Some showed me their cameras and seemed very polite. One dude shook his head up and

Moraine Lake
Banff - Canada

down, looking for my approval to take photos posing with La Loba. I consented with a friendly nod, and the man came fast and swung his leg on the bike. My pupils froze, I yelled a fierce< "No!" And pushed his ass off before he could even put his foot down. I looked at him square in the eyes, piercing every layer of his soul, dragging it out of his body, and gave it a good beating. He smiled nervously and did the head nodding thing again walking away. I honestly felt like a dick. I mean what's with the automatic nasty reaction? Why are we wired to not let anyone approach our bikes? Then I realized the answer was simple . . . because nobody fucking touches my bike! Period.

Stef came back more centered, her voice still with a crack. The solution was quite simple to get us going, we just needed a little muscle to push the bike and "clutch it." One of the hotel receptionists helped us move the massive 700-pound beast up a hill in the parking lot. We got the bike up, gasping for air. The thin air of the mountains had no mercy on my lungs. At the top I was spent, with both of my hands on my knees and with the tongue of a running chihuahua. I took a few deep breaths and grabbed the sissy bar on the back of the motorcycle, pushing as hard as I could. I pushed and ran with all I had. I yelled something guttural, as if I was in a battle scene from a Viking movie, where two clans are about to run toward each other, and some guy on the front lines raises his sword and yells some nonsense, and everybody gives it a run! The bike rolled down, and after picking up good speed, I yelled, "Now!" But to my dismay, nothing happened. I watched the Softail roll away from me without a jerk or cough at all. I was baffled and exhausted. I started to prepare mentally to sit there for a while, waiting for help to come to this remote part of the mountains.

Stefani was at the edge of bursting. I asked what happened. She said, "I don't know. I put it in gear as you told me and kept pressing the starter button as I rolled down, but nothing happened!"

I swallowed my reaction for a split second. My eyes were glassy as I stared at the horizon, completely numbed, trying to process the facts as my right eyelid twitched involuntarily. I took a big breath and realized that I had I assumed she would have known how to clutch the bike, so I didn't explain the full procedure to her ... my fault.

We rested for a minute and, once again, took on the ordeal of pushing the bike up the hill, which now seemed a few extra degrees steeper. This time we had the help of a trucker that was staying at the hotel. Stefani asked me to do it this time, and as I sat on her bike, I thought of the Chinese guy I denied touching my bike earlier. The gods were amused and giving me shit about my own arrogance, I'm sure.

The bike rolled down as I held the tall ape hangers trying to balance the beast. I waited to get enough speed and let go of the clutch, bringing it back quickly as the engine roared, jerking the entire bike frame. Our faces immediately lit up with excitement, and I gave the chromed machine a few celebratory loud revvings. The Chinese crowd clapped frantically, yelling some incomprehensible cheers and snapping what seemed like a terabyte worth of photos of us. I was now in full rockstar mode, with a ridiculous, over the top, tough face and awkwardly keeping it cool with a nonstop nod. For an instant, I was the unapologetic brown version of Brando in *The Wild One*, being there for half of my own movie with not many lines to say, just posing on every shot, looking good in a Schott jacket, yeah! For just that brief moment, I was that kind of cool. Finally, we packed everything back on the bikes, and again, twenty-three minutes later, we were back on the road to Jasper.

The road north was clear of traffic, the Rockies distilling its fresh air through the front opening of my helmet. I rode with the visor up and the guard down, moving easily along Alberta's well-kept black tops. The mountain range seemed to never end, creating a kinetoscope effect, a reiterative background moving by as I rode my bike through this great valley.

An unexpected, wide hairpin turn pointed my bike up, gradually climbing the highway up the mountains, leaving breathtaking images in my rear view mirrors. Looking back to the deepest part of the valley gave me a real sense of how

Columbia Icefield
Canada

big that country was and how relevant life feels there. Soon
we reached the Columbia Icefields, the largest icefield in
North America, wedged in the Canadian Rockies astride
the Continental Divide. The massive ice field covers part of
Alberta and British Columbia and has several glaciers.

The day was clear and sunny. Stefani and I decided to take a hike up to Athabasca Glacier. The path didn't seem difficult or far. But perception in those mountains is tricky. Boy, was I wrong! It didn't take long for me to realize this was a long trek. Of course, it was too late, as I had already done a quarter of the visible path. The incline got exponentially steeper, and my skinny calves were stretched to that point where my brain was hyper aware of it, sending neurotransmissions back in the form of "What the hell are you doing to your legs Miguel?!" I took it really slow, watching the local Canadian kids run past me. Stefani was so far ahead I could barely see her. Meanwhile, this tortured Latino soul was gasping for good old oxygen, and maybe a guava shake. I walked up in a zigzag pattern to soften the angle of the path and to adjust my breathing to the thin air.

Several signs on the eroded moon-like path marked where the edge of the glacier had been since 1890. It really shocked me how much of it had been lost forever in just recent times. The alarming note was that, in a matter of just a few decades, the glacier had receded at a rate of five meters per year, and Canadian Conservation Managers affirm the Athabasca Glacier could disappear within the next one or two generations.

The implications of drier times in the future and the rise of global sea levels because of the melting of the ice fields could be abrasive for our planet, and we must prepare for these changes. I have no intention to preach, but I feel politicians and all the sheep that follow them without questioning, consuming what they get on their TV sets as the absolute truth, those who negate the climate changes we as a human collective have created, all of them need to come out of their safe shells, travel, and see these palpable proofs of our actions. We all want to leave a better planet for our children, and as a father of two, seeing firsthand what science has been warning us about was an eye opener.

The melting of the ice caps, global warming, the bleaching of coral reefs, the indiscriminate deforestation, the accelerated extinction of many animal species; it's all real, I've seen it with my own eyes, I've experienced it firsthand on my travels. I say this to the non-science believers: just step outside, get off the damn couch and see for yourself, question it all . . . go travel! What you see in your favorite newscast and many shows on TV is no more than a "scripted reality," a convenient form of truth adapted to the interests of a few. I perhaps know a bit about this; I do have a communication degree, and I actually work in TV; but also, I've seen another reality as I exposed myself to different cultures and ideas from around our world. I say just try; open up your mind and judge for yourself.

Back on the bikes, I followed Stefani as best as I could. She can go steady at a buck forty without any flinch, as if she's going for a stroll in the park. Ripping at that many kilometers per hour on a motorcycle with no windshield makes everything in my peripheral vision become radially blurred. It's like travelling on a time warping tunnel, where an invisible force pushes my chest inward and my gripping hands are left numbed with no blood flow. I slowed down, trying to establish a long-distance tour pace, and followed Stefani the best I could. She was the little dot ahead taking a detour to visit Athabasca Falls.

We dismounted in the parking lot, and my arms dropped to the ground like a chimpanzee's. I swear my arms were about a foot longer. I checked La Loba, and she was perfectly in tune, with everything still in place. I quickly realized I was the only one falling apart, due to my still fragile stomach condition. I had to press on though.

Athabasca Falls is quite an impressive sight. The waterfall is, more or less, twenty meters high, but what makes it really admirable is the power of its waters. The wide and abundant Athabasca River converges into a limestone channel that is no wider than eighteen meters. The water funnels with immense pressure and violently drops into a narrow gorge, spraying the view with a glistening mist. The picturesque scene is surrounded by mountain peaks and the ever-present pines.

The mist suspended in the air is pierced by the sunlight, and sudden fractal rainbows appear at the base of the falls. The colors are intense. The raging white of the oxygenated waters turns gradually into a blinding cyan serpent disappearing down the deep gorge.

We arrived at the town of Jasper just past lunch time. We rode down the main strip and stopped to eat at the Jasper Brewing Company. I ordered a burger, something familiar. I asked it to be well done, not my usual taste, but I wanted to play it safe. I knew I needed a complete meal with plenty of proteins to push to Prince George that day.

Stefani and I were to split in Jasper; she was taking 93 back to Saskatchewan River Crossing and then 11 to Rocky Mountain House, and I was taking the Yellowhead Highway northwest. My idea was to push hard and reach Prince George that day, recovering some of the lost time. It was already past noon, so I knew I had to get moving soon and keep moving. We kept the farewell short and sweet. Little did I know it, it would be our last hug.

I'm grateful to have shared so many miles and stories with Stefani, a beautiful stubborn soul, a fighter, a living lesson of resilience, and a true caring woman, full of life and courage. Thank you for sharing your light. It was a blessing to know you.

SECTION VI

**ALBERTA - BRITISH COLUMBIA
CANADA**

PRINCE GEORGE

ALBERTA

JASPER

SASKATCHEWAN
RIVER CROSSING

BANFF

BRITISH
COLUMBIA

CANADA

THE SPILL

THE ANGELS OF PRINCE GEORGE

I kicked La Loba into sixth gear heading north on Highway 16, a road known as the Yellowhead Highway. Soon I crossed the border into British Columbia. I reached Moose Lake and entered Mount Robson Provincial Park. The highway path has the Rockies on one side and the Fraser River on the other. With every turn, the road offered an immaculate impression of natural beauty, putting my mind at ease.

The Yellowhead Highway threw me a wide turn, opening up to a majestic view of Mount Robson, a robust vertical mass of rock that makes up one of the tallest peaks in the entire region. The mountain elevates dramatically without any obstruction, showing the ripples and scars of time on its white face.

As Mount Robson lessened its size in my rearview mirror, I rode my way north, wedged in a valley of colossal peaks. Mount

Goslin, Mount John Oliver, Celtic Peak, Tindill Peak, were all looking down on my path and the road swerving at their feet.

Many "Falling Rock" signs decorated the highway, and the steep walls of stone were a bit intimidating. I saw an adult caribou grazing on the side of the road and slowed down and passed him carefully as he lifted his head and retreated rapidly into the woods.

I had one of those flash thoughts, a sort of premonition we all have from time to time on a motorcycle. I saw an image of me falling, an accident, a crash. I shook my head hard and shouted a very loud "¡A la mierda!" inside my helmet, a kind of "fuck that!" in Spanish. The road was desolate. There were only sporadic CanaDream RVs crossing paths with me here and there. The road lifted, and in a blind "S" turn, I suddenly hit a patch of loose rocks. I felt La Loba's tail going sideways, and I let go of the throttle and brakes, just keeping her square and softly counter steering to negotiate the second part of the turn without putting her to bed. She regained her center axis, and I pushed through slowly. My heart raced and the paranoia built up to a full tank. I passed a few goats doing suicidal jumps into the center of the road. I really needed to stop.

I pulled over at the town of McBride, filling up the tank at a Husky gas station. I stretched over a cup of coffee and let a few minutes pass to rest my body. I met a fellow biker at the pump who was crossing Canada in the opposite direction. He was riding a Frankenstein motorcycle he'd built himself with parts of different bikes. It looked pretty awesome, like a post-apocalyptic vehicle from the *Mad Max* movie. But my head was not really up for much talking. It was getting dark, and I still had two more hours of riding to reach Prince George. I was feeling tired but decided to continue.

I rode for about an hour, passing the Sugarbowl Grizzly Den Protected Area, and about half an hour later, I was crossing a small bridge over the Willow River.

It was getting pretty dark and started to rain lightly. I turn at the Willow River Rest Area to gear up for the rain. The tiny road has a steep incline, and as I went around the tight turn, I felt the weight of La Loba increase. We were going down. Eyes

The unfortunate consequence
of not listening to my body and pushing it too far

wide open, I grip the handlebars with all I have, pushing with my right leg to bring her back up, but the angle of the road won over my debilitated body, and then for the first time in all our time together, La Loba ate shit.

I jumped off the bike and rolled to avoid getting pinned under her on the incline, but by doing so I pulled my hamstring and felt the immediate and unmistakable piercing pain. La Loba was laying in the middle of the small road, taking so much space that no car would be able to pass. In the peak of the adrenaline rush, I tried to lift the bike by using one of those legs and butt pushing techniques I've seen in many motorcycle trade shows. I failed miserably. The motorcycle, being on a downslope, and the 600 plus pounds of metal was too much for my weak body, plus I could barely walk. I walked down toward the river and miraculously found a group of seniors travelling in a van. I asked them if they could help, and sure enough, the Canadian souls shined again. Two of the men and one of the ladies helped me bring La Loba back up. I put her on the kickstand and assessed the damage. The group of retired fellas took off, and I thanked them with a full open heart. I felt vulnerable. I was shocked and nervous, but mostly I was ashamed for letting this happen, pushing my body and mind so far.

I was told the stretch of road from McBride to Prince George is pretty much cursed, having the highest rate of moose collisions in the area. I had my taste of the curse in a different way, though. It started raining and getting dark. I was only half an hour away from Prince George and a safe place to get to. I decided to roll.

Since Jasper, I was exchanging texts with a friend from Instagram named Geoff. He was following my ride postings on the social media channel, and knew I had a hard time with my stomach in the past days and also that I was coming his way, but he didn't know of my accident.

With my leg cramped, I reached Prince George. Geoff was waiting patiently for me, sitting on his sweet Suzuki Boulevard motorcycle at a Petro-Canada gas station right at the outskirts of town. It was such a relief to finally get there and meet him. Even though I didn't know this man, I felt safe some how. I guess seeing his funny postings on Instagram for years somehow made him familiar.

Geoff is tall, with light blue eyes, a square jaw, and a blonde goatee. You could say he is the archetypal Canadian mountain man, with a wide strong frame, a constant smirk, and a silly sense of humor.

The moment I dismounted at the gas pump, we started laughing, and Geoff greeted me with a friendly biker hug, a welcomed sign in the motorcycle world that bonds unknown brothers and sisters. It's like a cult ritual, a card of acceptance, and for me at that moment I felt safe.

"Man, I was worried about ya!" he genuinely exclaimed. I explained my mishap dropping the bike and the reason why I was so late. Geoff asked me if I was okay to ride and to follow him, and said he had a place for me to stay.

We arrived at his house on a quiet suburban street. He mentioned how many bears roam the area. He opened the garage, and we pushed the motorcycles in. Right on the driveway sat a large RV, what they call a "Fifth Wheel." Geoff had it all hooked up for me to stay in. I couldn't believe his generosity! In the emotional state I was in, this was a humbling experience. I was vulnerable and with no option but to let myself be in the hands of this family.

I met his wife, Lisa, and his young son, and we chatted for a while, getting to know each other. We joked about people we knew on Instagram, motorcycle stories, and life. Lisa offered me coffee, and the warm cup felt fantastic in my hands. I sat in the living room on a plush, comfortable couch, and for an instant, it all went mute. My eyes wandered at a scene of laughs and smiles. The house, the kid, the pets, all the images in front of me were so familiar, yet so distant. My life once looked exactly like this: wife, kids, a beautiful Dutch Tudor house, a backyard with a wood deck and a grill. I used to sit on my own couch and let my best friend, Benito the Boston Terrier, jump on my lap, while watching my kids run around me. This, I once had.

I felt the contradictions of life hitting me in the chest. The ride had been long, and at the peak of exhaustion I'd gotten susceptible to the creeping thoughts echoing my past. Many times, I found myself comparing my path to the way my parents raised me. They were always there, together until the end, and they gave me all the basic tools I needed to succeed. I couldn't help feeling the weight of my own family life failure and went to a familiar emotional gutter, blaming myself for not being able to do the same with my own kids, at the same level. In my head, the echoing voice of my former wife began to read a stained eulogy for my role as a father, buried, incomplete, insufficient, and never good enough. My vision blurred as the tears built up in my eyelids. I shook the thought off with heavy effort. The volume in the room came back to normal, and I made a forced joke about their cat. "Hey, you know, I have an imaginary cat named 'Nipples'; Would you like to see photos of me playing with 'Nipples'?

I felt miserable. My tiredness was visible, and we called it off for the night. We went out to the RV, and Geoff gave me the rundown about the operation of the RV's light switches, the bathroom, and the doors. They even stocked the compact kitchen with some chips and snacks for my stay.

A few minutes later, as I was getting ready to lay down, Geoff came back with a tube of Voltaren, a medicated cream, to rub on my sprained leg and ease some of the muscular pain. I lay down on the bed, and in the solitude of the trailer, I had to remind myself that everyone has a unique journey to live, that the way I can support my children is just as good, as much as it is filled with love. I repeated to myself: "Love is always the answer." I faded rapidly and had a very pleasant sleep under thick comforters and with the smell of freshly laundered sheets.

The next morning, I woke up with Geoff knocking at the fifth wheel's door. He was bringing me a mug of fresh coffee, throwing me on a funky loop as he was recording a video with his phone, making jokes about what in hell I was doing with that Voltaren tube! The son of a gun even started a couple funny hashtags in social media: #prayformiguel and #miguellifematters as parodies of the popular support messages that are usually called out during major disasters.

It was a quiet Sunday morning, and I was mentally preparing to face the road again. But life has always something up its sleeve, and like a mind reader, Geoff gifted me with some more of that Canadian hospitality and compassion I'd experienced all across this land.

Miguel, sorry to tell you this, eh, but you're not going anywhere like this.
I'm just fine amigo, just a little more Voltaren and I'll be okay.
Sorry, but look at you, you can barely walk.
I don't want to make anyone uncomfortable man, I'll manage.
You're welcome here, sorry but you stay.

I knew I was not at a hundred percent, and a little bit more rest was most definitely the smart thing to do. So, I put my ego aside, and once again, let myself go with the fate of the journey.

Right on. Thank you so much, brother. If it's not an inconvenience I'd love to stay one more night in your RV. I truly appreciate it man . . . but hell you got to stop saying "I'm sorry."
Sorry—it's a Canadian thing.
No worries Geoff, all cool.
I'm sorry.
Okay stop that . . .

That Sunday we were supposed to ride for a little while, but the leg situation changed the plans. Geoff offered a wildlife sightseeing tour, so I plastered another layer of Voltaren on my leg and jumped in his pickup truck with my Nikon in hand to go on an impromptu photo hunt. We drove around the back roads of Prince George trying to spot the many bears supposedly inhabiting the area, at least according to Geoff, but curiously, not one bear showed up to the party, not even a deer, a chicken, or a stray dog. We even tried to take a couple dirt roads off the main paths, but came back empty handed.

We returned home without spotting any wildlife but made up for the day with good camaraderie and came back with an epic video of us singing the melody of the *Magnificent Seven* theme as we rode through the deep woods. Does anyone remember those fantastic Marlboro cigarette ads at the movie theaters, with cowboys, horses, aerial shots of the West, and that song blasting in all its glory?

That night I insisted on taking Geoff and his family for dinner. It was just a small gesture, compared to the generosity of their hearts and all they did for me in just a couple days. We went to a restaurant called the White Spot, a name I found really funny, as I realized I hadn't seen any brown homies in a while. "We Latinos don't like this cold weather, for sure," I laughed. The dinner was lovely, and I knew I had new friends for life and another true biker brother in Canada. We finished it off by taking a group photo with all of us flipping the bird "Motorwolf style."

That evening, Geoff and I sat down to discuss my route north. With my leg hurting, and after what I just went through, he was convinced I needed to reroute my journey. My original plan was to take Highway 16 toward Smithers and then north to Watson Lake. This route, though it has beautiful scenery, also has fewer towns, fewer people, fewer gas stations, and lots of unrepaired road areas, Geoff explained. He strongly suggested taking 97 north to Dawson Creek and to do the entire length of the famous Alaska Highway all the way north.

I had to trust my sagacious local friend and decided to take 97, as that route would provide me with more safety. I'd have a few more chances to refuel, and there would be more people around in case of a breakdown. I was starting to get a bit unsettled, as everyone pointed out that the road north would be difficult. Geoff warned me of long periods without seeing any traffic, long stretches in the absence of any gas, the wildlife on the road being way more active, the poor fuel quality, and the many road construction areas with frost heaves, loose gravel, and even the highway turning into dirt. I was queuing up for quite a treat.

I woke up early on Monday. Geoff was already up and helped me out with packing La Loba. "Here, take this, you're going to need it," he said, while handling me an extra fuel bottle. We had a brief farewell, and he went off to work. I felt great, rested, lucid, and ready to roll. I gave the map another glance, memorized the route, hit play on my "Motorwolf Rides" music playlist, and took off with AC/DC's "Highway to Hell" blasting in my helmet.

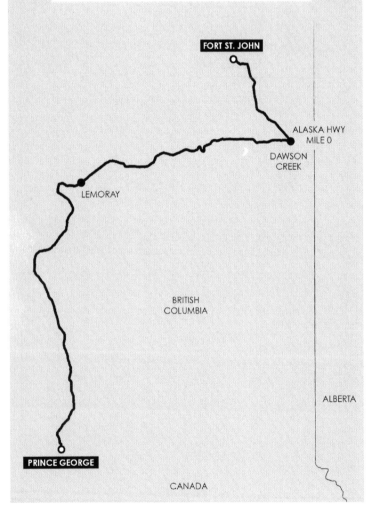

SECTION VII

BRITISH COLUMBIA
CANADA

FORT ST. JOHN

ALASKA HWY
MILE 0

DAWSON
CREEK

LEMORAY

BRITISH
COLUMBIA

ALBERTA

PRINCE GEORGE

CANADA

THE RED KEY

I jumped on the John Hart Highway with the headlamp pointed dead north and a full tank. I covered a good distance of pristine tarmac on my first leg, passing Beaver Creek and McLeod Lake. The highway distanced away from the tranquil waters, bearing toward the Rockies once again. The climb to Pine Pass is gradual and solitary, and a slight change in the temperature was noticeable. As I got near the higher altitudes of Pine Le Moray Provincial Park, the skies turned into a somber gray, the chilled air found its way through the cracks of my leather jacket, and a few rain drops hit my helmet visor. I slowed down, not bothering to suit on my rain gear. I just capitulated to the gelid rain, once again. A few kilometers ahead, I hit my first major Canadian road construction. Like everyone described, I had to be prepared to stay in line, usually in the middle of nowhere, and wait for a "Pilot Car" to usher me safely through the dirt and gravel stretches.

There were maybe nine or ten cars ahead of me. I stopped La Loba and put the kickstand down. An electronic road sign alerted me of twenty minutes of waiting time. "Well, look at this, how polite is this first world with its signage," I reckoned with a jaded sarcastic tone.

While sitting there looking at the surrounding sierra, a pickup truck stopped by me. The driver, I assumed by his dress code, was one of the engineers of the construction site. He rolled down the passenger window, and I felt the cool blow of conditioned air in my face. "Hello there, eh! Come follow me and drive your motorbike to the front, so when we start moving your bike doesn't get beaten by the rocks thrown by the cars in front of ya eh."

I shoved my sarcasm up my asterisk, realizing the genuine kindness Canadian people have in their ways. This was not Caracas anymore, I inevitably compared, a city where the latest generations have fully forgotten the beauty of courtesy and kindness. In Venezuela, nowadays, people come to a store with demanding language: "¡Dame una arepa de pabellón!" "Give me that, like now…" no good morning, good afternoon, a smile, a *please*. All the richness and beauty of the Castellano language seems to be fading into an arrogant collective that has forgotten to do good for others. But I suspect this is a deeper consequence of the many years of beatings sustained by a population led by an injurious system, one that promotes violence and favors maintaining people uneducated and misinformed.

At the front of the line there was a woman holding a "STOP" sign, I guess in her mid-twenties. She wore a safety fluorescent helmet and yellow shirt with reflective orange stripes. Her skin was pink by the exposure to the sun rays, and an unprovoked smile welcomed me to my new "pole position."

Hi, how long until the change?
Another ten minutes or so.
Well, good, I'm Miguel, by the way.
My name is Sarah … where are you from?
I'm from New York. I'm trying to reach Alaska.

Wow you're far from home, I used to live in Halifax, and now I'm here in the mountain side of the country. It's different, but I love it here, especially during . . . shhhhh . . . a hiss radio noise followed by a semi-clear voice came through her walkie talkie. She smiled and flipped the STOP sign to CAUTION, indicating us in line to proceed forward.

Sarah had a sweet smile, and in her voice I could sense the drive of a determined young woman. Our encounter was laconic, but the experience left me with an uplifted spirit, a lesson from an educated society, reflected by a chain of unpretentious acts of kindness.

I followed the pilot car slowly through what was now mud. They were going a bit too fast for my taste, but I didn't let the pressure of the cars behind bother me. I was really focused, gripping La Loba as straight as possible. I felt the motorcycle rear sliding sinuously to both flanks, and all I could do was to control her with my throttle while keeping myself centered and balanced. During the first stretch, I was passed by a few sand trucks and other heavy vehicles. I tried to get a good sense of the scene, knowing this would repeat itself many times on the road ahead.

I stopped after this first construction site experience to assess the damage. La Loba was covered in mud, with sandy streaks pushed by the water all over the exhaust pipes and the gas tank. The engine was beige, and her original denim black color had turned into a desert storm camouflage palette. I scraped off the mud from the air filter and verified all my levers were clear of dirt. I wiped off the thick mud from the headlamp, tail light, and turn signals. All my luggage was wet, and with not much else I could do there, I moved forward.

As scripted, I encountered many other construction sites of different lengths and with different levels of complexity. Some had loose gravel, some mud and downhills, some had really heavy machinery, some long waiting periods before letting me cross.

With all the rattling and shaking from riding over the dirt, the ever mysterious "red key" light on my speedometer lit up. "¡Coño! I've got a damn 'code'!" I couldn't believe my luck. "I must have a short somewhere, maybe a module was loose . . . " The "I'm alone in the middle of this hell" paranoia kicked in hard, and I resolved to keep an eye on the controls and to listen to the engine sounds. "C'mon baby! Keep it steady, take me there."

At the eastern bank of the Rockies I reached Dawson Creek. I knew this was an important moment of the ride when I passed the "Mile Zero" milepost, marking the beginning of the next fifteen hundred miles north to Fairbanks. I was now starting my journey to conquer one of the most gnarly roads in North America, the infamous Alaska Highway.

Road, sun, rain, mud, repeat. Me and La Loba accepted this equation for about five hours, and with the last bit of the second fuel tank of the day, I rode my last seventy kilometers to Fort St. John.

I was done with the dirt, the mud, the "follow me" trucks, and the rain, so I was in no mood for a camping site. I went straight for a clean hotel bed and paid the ninety bucks and change with gusto, all for the feel of clean sheets and a soft mattress to rest my back.

My body sank on the foam mattress. It felt heavy and immobile; involuntary tics moved muscles inside my calves, that made me giggle, since I had no power nor desire left to move at all. My body shut down and I woke up in the exact same position. I slept deep, with no dreams or thoughts left to recollect, only the marks of the sheets on my face and a trail of dry saliva were signs of my body's exhaustion. I went on with my morning routine and took a few minutes while packing the bike to pull the elastic band my physical trainer had given me back in Queens before the ride. I stretched for a few minutes, using the motorcycle sissy bar to attach one extremity of the elastic band to do some flexes. I'm not much of a gym guy so had no idea if I was doing the exercises properly, or if this had any impact at all on my body, so I quickly felt silly and went straight for something I knew would impact myself greatly: coffee and donuts.

I rode around the town looking for a place to clean La Loba, and a fellow biker directed me to Mic Suds Truck and Car Wash. The business had individual washing stations for pickup trucks, ATVs, cars, and motorcycles. The self-service operation charged by usage time. I scrubbed my bike vigorously and finished her with the pressure washer, getting rid of all the construction mud. She was back in shape . . . for now.

I found out there were no Harley dealers until Fairbanks, which was days away. I needed to deal with that "red key" light on La Loba's controls. I looked for any motorcycle shop or garage that could help me but without much luck. My only option in Fort Saint John turned out to be a Kawasaki dealer called Fast Trax. The guys were nice and helped me with my bike. Apparently, La Loba needed to get plugged in to be fixed, but the Kawasaki tech guy, who happened to ride a Harley, told me I would be fine riding like that.

It seems like the "red key" was just a disparity of voltage from my old turn signals to the new Kuryakyn LED lights I'd installed, so the bike was sending me a warning. The excess voltage would be resent back to the battery through the frame. Hey! Look at me talking like I know what the hell is going on. Regardless, my bike started and ran fine, so I was hitting the road again to get myself up to Fort Nelson.

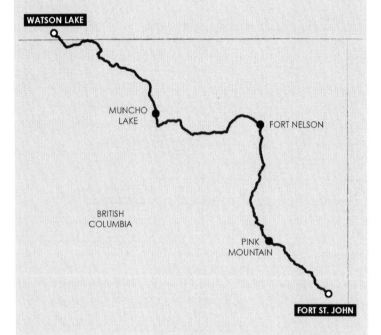

SECTION VIII

BRITISH COLUMBIA - YUKON
CANADA

YUKON

WATSON LAKE

MUNCHO
LAKE

FORT NELSON

BRITISH
COLUMBIA

PINK
MOUNTAIN

FORT ST. JOHN

CANADA

PURPLE RAIN

I stopped at an old gas pump on the outskirts of Fort Saint John to fill up La Loba and grab some snacks. The temperature dropped noticeably, and I knew of some mountain passes ahead, so I reached inside my luggage and grabbed my heated suit underlayer. I went inside the small convenience store, asking for the bathroom keys so I could change. The clerk appeared behind a wall of lottery scratch cards. She was an animated middle-age woman with quite a heavy body type, wild unbrushed hair, and no front teeth, which forced a phonetic hiss escaping from almost every syllable she pronounced.

Oh my Gosh, who are youz darling?
Aye . . . hi there . . . can I have the keys to the men's room please?
Baby, youz can haz the keyz of my house *if youz want!* She exclaimed while pointing at her crotch with both hands . . .

I swallowed hard and smiled politely as I grabbed the keys. I turned away and walked quickly to the back of the establishment, while the woman made at attempt to imitate cat purring sounds.

I stripped naked in the bathroom, balancing on top of my boots. I did my best to avoid the wet floor and managed not to fall over the dirty old mop or the toilet with no seat. I maneuvered around the molded walls and was somehow able to put on the long johns and the heated suit in that claustrophobic space, which I left smelling like Pinesol.

I threw the keys back at the counter as she kept making more blatant sexual epithets. I smiled and walked outside. I was both laughing at the scene but, at the same time, thinking how uncomfortable that made me feel. I stood by my bike reflecting on this single and rare incident for me, and quickly acknowledged this was the same incident that women across the world experience almost everywhere on perhaps daily basis. I thought of my daughter, her integrity and her safety. I exhaled in empathy, thinking how this small event in the middle of nowhere became a token of understanding for an issue I never paid attention to.

As I was about the head out, an all purple Harley-Davidson trike pulled over by the gas pump. The rider unmounted, revealing herself as a very friendly, mature lady in her mid- to late-fifties, I thought. Her hair was short and dyed bright purple, and she wore a purple shirt, jeans, and leather chaps.

Hi. I'm Sherry. Where are you heading?

I'm trying to get to Alaska. My hopes are to keep going north to the Arctic Circle.

That's wonderful; I'm heading to Alaska as well, but I'm going home, just north of Anchorage. I've been riding from Oregon.

By yourself?

Of course. Hey, if you want, we can ride together. It can get dicey up there with the rain and the construction.

For some reason, I declined Sherry's offer, even though it made so much sense to not be riding alone for the next stretch. She was from this part of the country and knew these roads well. I should have taken her advice, but the romantic notion of doing my own ride and dealing with every situation by myself was important to me. This was my own challenge, my own goals, my own stubbornness.

Sherry was just fine with my choice. She was also loving her own solo ride. We talked for a while and then took our own ways.

I jumped back on the AlCan, and soon the day unfolded as a carbon copy of the day before. I had to stop again and again at road construction sites, wait for the pilot truck to come and then follow its path, holding my bike with a death grip as the pilot truck led me through the irregular terrain of dirt and mud, and if I was lucky, through packed gravel.

I stopped at Pink Mountain for gas and some snacks. I wanted to pack plenty of water and power bars for the unknown ahead. The mirage of the unexpected was growing rapidly in my head. I couldn't shake the pressure, felt in the edge of my diaphragm, of the possibility of having a breakdown in the middle of that remote area of the continent. Also, I was petrified with the notion of encountering a bear and my bike not responding.

The Alaska Highway grew in desolation. The sky was sharp blue, and the wind felt cold. The roughness of the road suddenly dissipated, offering a ubiquitous silence, solely perturbed by the sporadic log truck, with their rattling roar, leaving a shower of debris on their way.

I came across my first large Caribou sighting. As I swiftly came through a wide open turn, the young bull was by the edge of the asphalt. His bravado and curiosity kept him by the road, forcing me to slow down quickly as a precaution. I couldn't really tell what he was about to do, but as I got closer, he ran back into the shrubs. I slowed down enough so that I was able to capture a photograph of the reindeer and knew these events with the northern fauna would become more reiterative.

As predicted, later that day, I got stopped again by animal traffic. This time by a herd of mountain bison lying on the road. There I was, remembering their cousins from Yellowstone, with their same "we don't give a fuck" attitude, taking in all the warmth of the road. This time the difference was that not a single human soul was around, not a car to jump to or a place to run. I quickly devised my own plan for these encounters with animals larger than me. I figured it was wise to stop my bike in a half-profile angle, instead of facing straight at the animals. This plan served two purposes. On one hand, it made me look larger to the animal, hence a bit more intimidating. On the other hand, being at an angle allowed me to turn my bike back quickly and have a way out in case any of these beasts felt a burst of temerity and charged me.

I sat there for quite a while. A few of the bison were lying flat, comfortably on the road. I understood it was siesta time. I didn't want to mess with that. I knew the consequences very well. I remember waking up my mom once from her siesta and getting a good "chancletazo." Oh, the chancleta! That terrifying sandal, a flying flip-flop thrown by Latino moms like GPS guided missiles, always accurate to land a stingy slap on the back of their children's necks.

A small sedan appeared in front of me, coming from the opposite direction. He started flashing the car's headlights, and the scene turned quite laughable. The bison were not conceding their claimed piece of tarmac. It took an eighteen-wheeler's loud honk to move the herd away.

The path cleared, I moved easily, passing the dust and sweat of the bison's stampede. From there, the road glided among mountains of capricious shapes. I lost count of the many rivers and lakes my eyes flirted with and was enamored with the colors of the deep northern forests. I caught myself becoming a sort of rare nemophilist, in total ecstasy, fed by cobalt blue waters, raw umber rocks, and the dark green of the conifers.

That portion of the Alaska Highway felt magical, as if the laws of the universe were challenged. I was still, my hands were locked in the same position, the vibration vanished, the bike immobile, and the hissing sound of the wind dissipated. I felt halted in time and space and it was the road and scenery that were moving toward me. Like a scene from a science fiction movie when a spaceship enters warp speed, I felt I was moving through my own panoptic projection.

I arrived that afternoon at Fort Nelson, a small town encrusted in Canada's boreal forest. There was not much energy left in me and not much to see anyway, so I went straight to find food and a place to spend the night. I stopped at a Super 8 motel with a Boston Pizza restaurant next to it. It served the purpose, and the price was good, applying some of the coupons I had collected on the way. I sat at the bar and went for the chicken wings platter and asked for a Molson Canadian. The bartender was a good looking, all Canadian woman, remarkably blonde, in her late twenties, I presumed, with a sculpted body and the curves of the "Tail of the Dragon." Her blue eyes were bright and alive, and she carried a smile that brightened the entire hall. Next to me was an older guy, perhaps my age. He spoke French while chewing nachos at the same time. He was wearing a gray suit, portraying a businessman on a trip. The francophone was being very forward with the bartender. His conversation was prosaic and turned borderline rude as he tried to compliment the girl. The girl kept smiling, and at that point I knew it was forced. I realized this businessman was no better than the stereotypical catcaller at a construction site, or perhaps the lady back at the gas station in Fort Saint John.

I was tired, and for a moment it all began to blur together in a train of thought. I paused; something bothered me about the scene beyond the obvious. I then realized I was comparing it to the realities of my upbringing. Latin American men get a bad reputation as "machistas" and catcallers. As a Venezuelan man, I'm thrown into that pile. But the more I travel this so called "First World," the more I see the same exact behavior in many men. They are no different. It seems clear to me that this issue is beyond ethnicities or socioeconomic labels. The Molson tasted flat, so I went to bed.

In the morning, I was examining the breakfast lounge, deciding between scrambled eggs and Fruit Loops, living my very old internal debate about "adulting" or not. A man noticed the small flags sewn on the back of my vest and politely inquired about them with lively curiosity. I explained those were the flags of the countries I'd ridden on motorcycles so far. With an open display of wonder, he asked, "Is that the Venezuelan flag?" I was impressed; it's not often I come across people with a good knowledge of geopolitical symbols. He invited me to join him and his family at the table, introducing me to his wife.

Then it all became clear to me," ¡Hola, mi nombre es Alejandra; yo soy venezolana!" Exclaimed the South American lady. I was perplexed to meet a Venezuelan this far north on the planet. Those encounters were rare in those latitudes, I reckoned, so we started a desperate exchange of a meaningless conversation filled with heavy "caraqueño" versus "maracucha" accents. I burst out the gooey Spanish from Caracas, while she made a loud display of the way the language is spoken in Maracaibo, the two largest cities in Venezuela, now filling the middle of the Canadian North with its sounds. We chatted of nothing in particular. The obvious need was to expulse as many colloquial words from the Bolivarian republic as we could, like a relieved pressure valve. Not seeing Venezuelans at all for so long, made us both speak a rapid-fire spill of chamos, vainas, chéveres, carevergas, and many Venezuelanisms.

After a few intense minutes of overlapping each other with outdated Venezuelan words, we both exhaled with an orgasmic grin on our faces. The husband had absolutely no idea about what was going on. He politely smiled and sensed the cathartic energy flowing from us, witnessing one of the tragedies of us immigrants. Then the cursed topic that follows every Venezuelan began. The husband, trying to join the conversation, started talking about the radical socialist regime and the political atmosphere in the South American country, all faces instantly became somber, and before letting anyone ruin my day, I interrupted, "Oh well, it's getting late, I must be on the road . . . ¡Adios amigos!"

It was another immaculate day, with a glorious bright sky and a comfortable temperature for riding. At least with that I'd been particularly lucky for the most part. I left Fort Nelson a little earlier than usual, since I knew I had to do yet another mountain pass that would slow me down. After a few kilometers riding by the side of the Tetsa River, I sure noticed when the relief of the Northern Rocky Mountains showed up near Stone Mountain Provincial Park. La Loba started to climb the mountain pass toward Toad River. The Alaska Highway became narrow and curvy. I rolled down my right hand, slowing the motorcycle in case of a sudden loose gravel segment. I kept an eye on the edge of the road, with its intimidating unfenced drops. I felt the back of the bike slip a couple times. I needed to be one hundred percent focused on the road, every crack, every patch or change of pavement color, every pebble, or worse, every frost heave could be a potential disaster.

I crossed a few metal-grated bridges with grooves so wide that it made the bike feel like it was going sideways, almost as if the bike had its own mind. I really had to pull her square like a reigned wild mustang to control my direction on those bridges. One quickly learns how that highway has something up its sleeve for every traveler.

I reached Toad River at the 422 mile marker of the Alaska Highway. I unmounted the bike, without having seen any human at all on my path so far that morning. The lodge at Toad River was a nice welcomed sight. It was already lunchtime, and I went inside their singular restaurant, decorated with the world's largest collection of baseball caps and trucker hats. The collection was started in 1979, and they claim to have over 7,200 hats tacked to the restaurant ceiling. The colorful and entertaining decor was just fine in which to relax and let some time pass. I sat and devoured a "Bear Paw" burger with a Coke.

I learned the Toad River got its name from the times when the Canadian and US Army were building the highway back around 1942. The river at that location had no bridge built yet, so most vehicles needed to be towed. Apparently, the owners of the lodge decided to name it "Toad River Lodge," mistakenly thinking they were calling it "Towed." This reminded me of a tale back in the marine port of Maracaibo, where they tell the story of a woman infatuated with the men aboard an American frigate. She named his son Usnavi, after hearing these men were the "U.S. Navy."

I filled up the tank, $14.85 Canadian Dollars, at the time, about $11 US Dollars more or less. As I stood there holding the fuel nozzle, I heard the rumble of the dazzling purple trike of Sherry. "There she is!" We winked at each other once more with a brief hello, just a small sign that reaffirmed our journeys. I'm not sure why, but even though we were doing our own separate rides, somehow that little wink made me feel I was not alone. I realized the lonely road was taking a psychological toll on my mind, and I was clinging to any sign that would give me the courage to continue.

With a filled-up tank and a filled-up stomach, I moved on. Cruising the northern lands of British Columbia was seductive; the forest monologue of fir and rocks slowly swallowed me whole. It had been another hour on the road when I made it to Muncho Lake. The highway gradually became scarred, with a broken and undefined edge, full of loose gravel and small weeds finding their way resiliently through the rocks. The appearance of the road gave it a more desolate feel, an eerie form of abandonment.

I passed what appeared to be a rustic landing strip for small airplanes, then the saturated blue waters of Muncho

Lake came into view. I pulled over to photograph the serenity of the place. The silence was remarkable, disrupted only by the occasional breeze blowing in my ear. I expanded my lungs deeply, and the blood vessels in my nostrils froze, provoking an electric tingling sensation radiating up to my eye sockets and my head. My eyes watered lightly as I quieted my mind into this place. I sat on La Loba for a good fifteen minutes, facing the lake and with the road behind me. The surrounding mountains reflected on the lake, giving a darker shade to its waters. But the near shore quickly turned into a translucent emerald green, revealing the many pebbles of the lake floor. The Alaska Highway runs for about thirteen kilometers on the eastern edge of the lake, unfenced and raw. I sat there, alone. Just there, I lived.

The passing of a couple RVs, followed by a few cars trying to pass them, interrupted my awakened trance. I chewed on one of the power bars I carried inside my top bag and drank half a bottle of water, before jumping back in the saddle. I rode further north, mirroring the Liard River course. For about two hundred kilometers, I danced with every turn and twist of the river banks. Nothing but immeasurable trees, mountains, open skies, the empty road, the occasional bison, and wait! Is that Sherry on the purple trike passing me again?

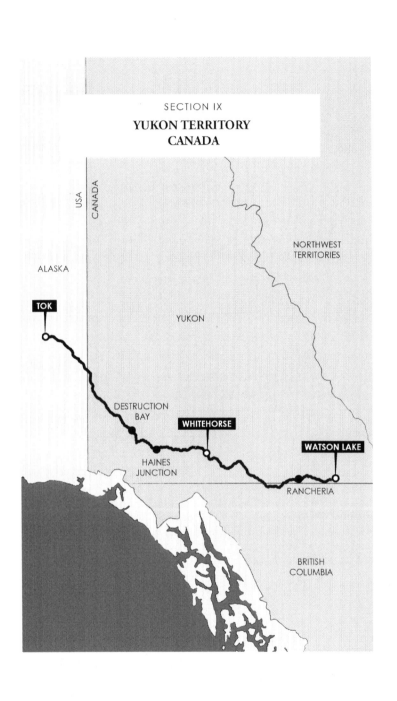

SECTION IX

YUKON TERRITORY
CANADA

USA

CANADA

ALASKA

NORTHWEST
TERRITORIES

TOK

YUKON

DESTRUCTION
BAY

WHITEHORSE

WATSON LAKE

HAINES
JUNCTION

RANCHERIA

BRITISH
COLUMBIA

LARGER THAN LIFE

SURVIVING YUKON TERRITORY

The road unbent into a long stretch, and I opened the throttle, savoring the winds and perhaps the few bugs in my teeth. At the end of the stretch there was a large sign with uncomfortable blue letters that said, "YUKON" in a condensed serif font. Underneath it read, "LARGER THAN LIFE," and further down the equivalent French "PLUS GRAND QUE NATURE." I stopped to flip the bird at the sign and to take my customary photo. The place was quiet, and the chirp of crickets was, not figuratively speaking, it was literally all I heard. It sunk in. *I* was entering the Yukon Territory—I was far from home, so fucking far!

The AlCan wove in and out, between the Yukon and British Columbia. The ride was relaxed and still under clear skies. That day I reached Watson Lake, still in mid-afternoon, and decided it was time to stop. I glanced at the first motel

I saw along the road and went straight to it. It was not a corporate chain hotel, so I bet it would have a decent price. The Andreas Hotel was all I needed: a family owned place, clean, and comfortable. The lobby had a couple red couches, an ATM machine, the heads of a bear and a ram goat on the walls, and a friendly lady behind the desk. My room was at the end of a hallway covered with a floor-to-ceiling wallpaper of a forest. Going to and from the room felt as if I was walking through the woods.

Right away, I went out for an early dinner. I wanted to wake up the next day at the crack of dawn to make sure I would have enough riding time in daylight. I rode around and quickly recognized Sherry's purple bike parked in front of Kathy's Kitchen. The sign above the wooden building read, "A little taste of home." I was absolutely sure they didn't have any Venezuelan arepas, nor New York bagels, but I went in to share time with my fellow traveler and to definitely try some of that "taste of someone else's home."

Sherry was sitting outside on the front porch of the restaurant. She was sharing a table with a man who introduced himself as Dewey, a member of the official Harley Owners Group of Alaska.

Dewey and Sherry shared stories from local motorcycle rallies and talked of people they knew in the biker community. I listened, not interjecting much. I wanted to learn more about this brave woman, riding solo in those latitudes. Dewey left soon after I finished my meal, then Sherry told me about what it means to live in Alaska. It was clear to me Alaskan people were made different, more rugged and frontal. My first impression was that Alaskans are the type of people that get shit done, that don't beat around the bush, and instead are very direct and raw. I liked it and identified with their ways. The sun burned a mirage on the horizon, and we stared at the fading of another day. I snapped a couple photos of Sherry and her purple motorcycle against the glorious sunset, and then went back to my motel, immensely inspired by the calmed determination and sense of power that Sherry had.

Yukon
Canada

I lay down in my bed, thinking. I was about to head north into the Yukon, a massive territory sparsely inhabited by about 35,000 people all together; 24,000 of those people living in Whitehorse, the only city in the entire territory. I'd learned the Yukon population density is 0.18%, which means there isn't one person per square mile, not even *one* soul. All sorts of scenarios ran through my mind, like getting a flat or a mechanical failure in the middle of nowhere, or worse, getting into an accident this far from everything I know. It seemed to me this vast land was just ideal for making anyone "disappear," so my Caracas survivalist sense got in full effect. And how about a bear encounter? I thought of that almost every day after my first bear sighting back near Prince George. Just the thought of bumping into a brown bear paralyzed every single fiber of my nervous system.

The next morning, I set my goal to reach Whitehorse. I sat at Andrea's restaurant and ordered my usual breakfast of runny eggs, bacon, and a half stack of pancakes. I doubled up on coffee and took off.

Just a few blocks away, I encountered the famous Sign Post Forest. This landmark of the AlCan contains a large collection of signs that extends over two acres. I walked through this maze discovering posts from all over the world, including license plates, street signs, welcome signs, and distance panels.

The Sign Forest was started by an American soldier during the construction of the road, back in 1942. He was assigned to repair a sign post that indicated distances, so he decided to customize it by adding his hometown in Illinois. Since then, roughly over 100,000 signs have been added.

I entertained myself, looking at the designs of all the post signs, some of them coming from as far away as Australia and Germany. I found an open spot and tagged it with a Motorwolf decal for posterity and to mark my travels. I looked at my little company logo amid a sea of signs and felt we were part of something big. I smirked and rolled back to the AlCan, which, changed its name to Highway 1 once I crossed into the Yukon.

About a couple hours into the ride, I spotted a nice café called Ranchería. The place even had a gas pump, which was a great relief, since my concern for finding fuel was increasing exponentially to paranoiac levels. I wanted to top the tank off at every chance I'd have. Ranchería seemed to be in the middle of nowhere, but somehow it made total sense. The desperate need for a break with the reassuring comfort of a cup of coffee, and perhaps a bite of one of their pastries and on top of that being able to get gas made the place the perfect oasis on that lonely road. I was now standing on mile 710 of the Alaska Highway. What felt like an eternity was not even halfway to Fairbanks.

That afternoon I made it to the small town of Teslin. I took a break at the Yukon Motel and Restaurant, located right off the main road. I bought some snacks and a bottle of water and stood at their deck stretching my legs and popping some trail mix. I saw a sign for a "Wildlife Exhibition" at the next building. The entrance had a large stuffed toy of a moose welcoming the visitors. I found it childish, making me hesitate amid my testosterone fueled adventure; but the good old "Free" sign lured me in very quickly.

The exhibition turned out to be quite good, with well-curated scenes from the Canadian wilderness. Large taxidermy struck dramatic poses depicting the way animals survive in those latitudes. The dioramas were finished with natural props and painted backdrops of mountains and open skies. Arctic foxes, owls, bears, and caribou were all represented. But the most impressive piece in the exhibition was a scene of a large bull moose being attacked by wolves. The massive moose looked down with a mix of fear and resignation, as two wolves ran surrounding him, ready to strike. The violent scene, capturing the fragile instant that separates life and death, had my complete attention. At that split second, we will all face at the end of our times, beyond material possessions, vanity, achievements, power, love, origin, skin color, and all we know.

The moose and the wolves reminded me of Venezuela, my upbringing, the struggles, the ambitions, and the invalidated outcome of everything. The diorama had a plaque that read:

> *The Last Morning: A simple act of survival, played out each day in the wilderness. No victim and villain, but components in nature, and for all, even the mighty and the clever, there will be a last morning.*

I left Teslin with a sour feeling but somehow with a renovated determination to continue forward in whatever "morning" this was for me. As a solo long-distance rider, I feel I play a staring contest with the ripper every time I swing my leg over the bike. But instead, the lurking notion of death motivates me to be present and live that moment in full. I plugged in my iPhone and blasted Airbourne's "Runnin' Wild," shook off the mental distractions with a couple revs, and thundered my way to Whitehorse.

The clock ticked 7:30 that early night, but the light of the day was putting on a good fight. The sky was gray and cloudy, and the wind felt cold. I entered Whitehorse, and the act of riding in a larger city caught me by surprise. I quickly had to focus and adapt to the higher volume of traffic, dealing with the daring intersections of the city. I realized how comfortable I'd been on the open road and how cities made me feel drained in just a few minutes.

With a population of just about twenty-five thousand, Whitehorse is the only "city" in the Yukon. I figured this was the most people I would see for a couple days. As we say in Venezuela, after Whitehorse it's all just "monte y culebra." I guess this translates somewhat into "grass and snakes," which is all too wrong for these mountains, but saying "fir and deer" just didn't cut it for me.

I woke up to an ominous gloomy day. It was cold, and the sky was washed with an apocalyptic shade of gray. It rained during the night, and I had to go over the duties of drying the seat, wiping the mud off the bike controls and lights, cleaning the air filter, and checking the brakes.

While the average temperature in the Yukon Territory during the winter months is mild by arctic standards, there's

Somewhere near Rancheria
Yukon

no other place south of the arctic in North America that gets as cold. I learned the most extreme cold recorded there was in

February 1947 when the abandoned town of Snag dropped down to −63.0 °C (−81.4 °F). Of course, I was riding in late August, so I was not even near such temperatures, but my Caribbean bones were definitely feeling the cold air and the rain.

I was told the next stretch of road was pretty much "in maintenance," and for the next couple days there would be no other sign of civilization, other than the road and a couple gas stations. I made a few planned stops before leaving Whitehorse and "civilization" for that reason. First, I topped off the gas tank. I went a little over the usual limit and spilled some of the gasoline over the tank. My hand shook, realizing I was both nervous and cold. I also filled both my emergency fuel bottles and strapped them to the bike's frame. Later, I stopped at a Staples store to buy a sharpie. I was now closing on the Alaskan border, and I had this idea to draw a big "50" in my hand to flip the bird once I reached the welcome sign of the last frontier state. Riding in Alaska would be of great significance for me. By doing so I would then have ridden in all of the fifty states of the American union.

The rain started to fall again. The forecast called for showers all day. I suited up with my obnoxious rain gear in the Staples parking lot. As I awkwardly tried to pull up the synthetic pants, an archetypal cougar, by popular definition, walked by and looked at me with disgust. "Freak," she mumbled. Then as she kept moving, she flipped her hair with an exaggerated head turn and look back, with a smirk that one can assume she had practiced for years in front of her bathroom mirror, imitating an ad for some shampoo brand. I smiled at her in embarrassment and kept pulling, shaking my butt, and jumping to fit into my pants. The neon yellow color of the rain jacket was perfect, not just to keep me dry, but to make me visible to others in such dim conditions. I checked my bike's headlight and my hazard signals and found them to be in good standing, I adjusted my balls and slowly let go of the clutch.

I went extra easy on the throttle, hoping to stretch my fuel range. The rain made things worse, slowing me down even more. The road became muddy and loose under La Loba. A terrifying tint of slate gray permeated the thick collection of cumulus clouds above me.

One hour into my day's ride, I was crossing the mountains along the Champagne and Aishihik First Nations lands, when the motorcycle shook with a violent cough, discharging a misfire explosion out of her pipes. La Loba was suddenly losing power, rattling every time I went up the rolling hills. The bike trembled under me with a stuttering tachycardia, and out of panic, I pressed harder on the throttle to try to keep momentum. Somehow the trick worked, and I kept the bike rolling. An old pickup truck was following close behind, and they never bothered to pass my erratic motorcycle. I felt a bit safer having the truck in my rearview mirror; it was a sign of available help if my bike died.

"¡Vamos carajo!" I yelled all sorts of Spanish curses and begged La Loba not to break down. I was visibly nervous. I kept pushing the throttle and dealing with the consequences of the sudden acceleration on the rainy and muddy conditions. The bike's rear tire was spinning loosely at each of her sudden coughs, and right-hand control became the factor between moving forward or having my face splattered in the mud. My left hand was bouncing between a firm grip on the handlebars, trying to keep the balance, and letting go of it to wipe my helmet visor of the thick rain drops.

It took me an eternity to reach the next town. It felt as if I was crawling through those hills. When the sign of Haines Junction came in sight, I felt a great relief. I needed to stop and take a break from the first battle of what would become the toughest couple days of my trip.

I pulled over at a Shell gas station, close to where the road continues as Alaska Highway and splits with the Haines Road. I filled the tank once again with some mystery gas, and then it hit me, perhaps that was the cause of my bike intermittently losing power. But there was nothing I could do. Here you get to fill up with whatever piss you find. The guys in the pickup truck pulled in behind me. They were two men in their fifties, wearing plaid flannel and working boots. "You were having a rough one out there, eh!" exclaimed the driver. I smacked my lips with indifference and exhaled a long "yep." I was too tired to engage in a small talk and in no friendly mood. "We saw you losing speed back in the hills," he continued, as I nodded with a prosaic enthusiasm. I just needed to be left alone to think about my safety and next move. The driver casually went on talking " . . . So, with the rain and all that, we decided not to rush and to take our time to escort you, in case you broke down, my friend. Glad you made it." My mind went blank, my shoulders fell to the ground, and my lungs emptied at once. I felt like shit.

Once again, the tough lone wolf I had taught myself to be was standing face to face with wolves of pack mentality. The illusion of biker clichés cross-faded into a reality I was quick to learn. People are intrinsically good, and it's only conditioning that warps that truth. My resolution of learning from my traveling was strongly founded on the pragmatic idea of keeping an open heart to the world. And this was another corroborating lesson for my idea of living; another transformative moment learned from motorcycle travelling. I apologized to the men for my attitude and thanked them genuinely for their gesture and their compassion.

I walked across the street to a roadside motel and asked the front desk attendant if she could point me to a garage or any mechanic who could check on my motorcycle. Like most women in those latitudes, she was versed in matters of a mechanical nature. I'm quite sure she could have done the job herself and told me to shut up and learn. She was a modern-day Rosie the Riveter, bold, and confident, beautiful in her own way. Unquestionably, she pointed me in the direction of a local garage up the road.

I rolled into a place called Kluane Machine, just off the highway. There was a sign that read "Auto, RV and Trailer Repair." I felt a slight comfort hoping I would find the help I needed with La Loba. The entrance was a large gravel lot with a few cars and tractors randomly parked here and there. There was a blue-gray industrial-looking building, but the main gates were closed. I went inside through a small side door I saw cracked open. "Hello! Anyone? Hello!" Silence. The garage felt orphaned at that hour. A sudden clunking sound of metal being dropped on the floor startled me, my alert senses went on, and I took a quick look at everything around me in a futile attempt at hyper-awareness. Then a small figure of a man appeared from behind a Chevy truck on a lift, his face covered in black tar and dust, his hands gripping a large wrench. "How can I help you?" the silhouetted man exclaimed as he walked toward me. Ahem! Ehhh . . . open heart Miguel, open heart I thought. " . . . well my motorcycle seems to be losing power, and perhaps you could take a look and help me find out why that is?" "What kind of bike is it?" "It's a Harley sir". He grunted and came out to see the bike. After running the bike and doing some routine checks, the initial assessment was that I needed to replace the spark plugs. But he didn't have such plugs, and it would take at least three days to get them up there at "The Junction," as locals called their town.

I couldn't afford three days of waiting, so I cleaned up the air filter and the plug's contacts myself. I tried to remove as much mud and dirt off the engine and electrical parts. I checked my brakes and decided to give it a go. As I walked out, the man gave me his business card. Mike was his name. He left me with the impression of being a very laconic man. I felt the only affinity between us was perhaps just the name, not much else.

I thought of the poor quality fuel I was feeding La Loba and mentioned it to Mike. He had a bottle of octane booster bottle I could buy. I added a couple ounces to the tank and crossed my fingers, firing the bike on. Brooom! The bike started immediately. After several minutes, the engine seemed smoother. The cocktail was doing the job, optimizing the gasoline, and I was ready to keep burning it.

The rain stopped for an instant, and I took that as a cue to continue with my journey ahead. I rode, flanked by Mount Martha and the Kluane National Park. About an hour and a hundred photos later, I came into a wide turn that opened up into some sort of a bay. The large body of water of Kluane Lake took over the landscape on my throttle side; on my clutch side the sun was breaking through gunmetal clouds, shooting down an overlay of sun rays, burning the water surface into hundreds of blinding, glimmering strokes.

The road took me across a long bridge, where the silver waters of the Slims River flow into Kluane Lake. It looked like the bridge was the limit between good and evil; on one side the rainstorm retreating into the sierra, on the other side a bright blue sky revealing all the splendor of Sheep Mountain in front of me. At the end of the bridge there was a large rest area with a spectacular view of the lake, and tucked under Sheep Mountain was a visitors' center as well. The mountain, known by the natives of the area as Tachäl Dhäl, has one of the largest concentrations of wild sheep in Canada.

I was happy to stop and wipe the bike of debris and mud. The weather changed drastically, and a patch of blue sky opened up amidst the storm. I rested a little longer than usual. Despite the good signs of the weather, a stream of negativity poured through my mind. I had to fight the thoughts of being cold, being wet, the road conditions, and my physical weakness due to the recent stomach virus, and my fucked-up leg. I was trying hard to rest for a few minutes, yet was invaded by thoughts of me falling again, and the lurking prospect of a major accident. I looked around. It was empty, wide open. I felt alone. My fears were telling me there was nothing in that place and to move on; and on the other hand, my courage was reassuring me that this place, this moment, had everything I wanted: life, experience, adventure.

I rode the dramatic shoreline of Kluane Lake and found myself in late afternoon in a minuscule place called

Destruction Bay, population fifty-six. There was The Talbot Arm, a small roadside motel on mile 1083 with clean basic accommodations; a convenience store that also functioned as the motel front desk; a modest restaurant with a nice view of the lake; a lounge; a cafeteria; and best of all, the place was also a Fas Gas station. It was a form of mountain wilderness oasis, and for a few Canadian dollars I was booking myself a much needed room and a shower.

I slept like a bear and woke up earlier than usual to a quick meditation routine, a simple thing I'm not good at but try to practice to keep the synchronicity of mind and body. I meditate to quiet my thoughts and keep my travels grounded, connected to the elements. As I said earlier, I'm not a religious man, although I grew up in a strong Catholic family. I abandoned those beliefs once I reached the age of reason. I don't chant ohms, neither do I preach about chakras, apostles, dudes being swallowed by whales, dudes walking on water, UFOs, vegan food, CrossFit, or holy lands. But one thing is certain, my lack of believing in the imaginary narratives of organized religions or dogmas doesn't push me away from my own spirituality. I believe in Nature:

Nature is my religion, Mother Earth is my church, and riding is my prayer.

The Worst Is Yet to Come

I sat at the Talbot Arm restaurant and ordered a half-stack of pancakes, coffee, orange juice, bacon, and two eggs over easy. Talking to the waitress, I learned Destruction Bay apparently got its name during the construction of the highway. It is said the winds here constantly blew away the buildings made by the military. She was emphatic when she told me it was a challenge to live there. Her words reminded me that I haven't had any arepas in weeks, so I sympathized with her angst. "Yeah, it must be hard," I exhaled.

That day my goal was to get to the Alaskan border and reach the town of Tok. It was about 7:30 in the morning. I was completely flabbergasted I was up and ready that early, but excited and anxious to reach my goal of riding in all of the fifty states of the USA . . . and now the border was a day of riding away.

At the gas pump there was a man with a thick white mustache wearing a wide brim hat of the same color. I thought he looked like a character from a television series from the

'70s, a Burt Reynolds of sorts. He was filling up his small RV and said he was coming from Alaska with his family, while looking at my beaten and dirt covered Harley. He was intensely staring at the dollar numbers going up at the pump, mechanically flipping with a clicking sound. There was a long pause, his head tilted and his lips flattened under the mustache. Then he broke his self-imposed silence with a single dooming statement "... the worst part is yet to come, son." I waited for the Western movie shoot-out scene tension chords to come out of nowhere, but only the ticking of the pump was heard, then silence—another long pause.

Apparently, the road from Destruction Bay all the way to the United States border was a complete disaster. He gave accounts of at least three major road construction sites and told me one of them ran for about forty miles. In his nicotine infused voice, and with a particular inflection at the end of his sentence, he warned me to be extra careful, since they were grading the road up there. I was soon to learn the meaning of that.

Kluane Lake shrunk in my right-side rearview mirror. The mountains were washed with a veil of ivory mist, and the view through my helmet had a dull matte feel. The scenery looked like it was posted by a hipster's Instagram account, with that trendy faded look. The petrichor was strong; my nostrils dilated with the smell of fir. Light rain conditions were forecast for the whole day, keeping my left hand busy wiping the resilient raindrops off my visor. La Loba was running smoothly, and the engine felt quiet after another dose of the gas booster. I realized I had a tight grip on the bike. I was tense.

Midnight Oil's "Beds are Burning" kicked in on my music playlist, and I gained a fierce boost of confidence. I'd been a fan of the band since 1987, when I got my hands on their *Diesel and Dust* record that had immediately impacted me. Coming off an era dominated by shredding guitar solos, long hair, and cheesy ballads, Midnight Oil's music shook my world. The politically infused lyrical work and the cleaner sound of their guitars broke the status quo in the times when music was still shaping my persona. I admired Peter Garrett as a musician and for his political involvement in Australia; but also, Jim Moginie and Martin Rotsey guitar arrangements. They were a strong influence in my later music career and the way I developed my own guitar style when my band got signed by Warner Music.

Small orange flags by the side of the road marked the areas where sudden potholes or rough patches began. The AlCan felt heavy and rougher, giving the motorcycle a chronic vibration. I felt the tiny waves rebound in every corner of my body. I'm sure my sperm count was taking a nosedive, and often I had to stand on the motorcycle pegs to give my family jewels a break.

The first couple gravel patches weren't that bad, I guess they were the warm-up for the challenges ahead. Things began to get difficult when I reached what I believed was Pickhandle Lake. The gravel got deeper and dense, and all the effort handling the motorcycle was concentrated on keeping it square as the tires fell into the deep grooves of pebbles. "Don't fight it, Miguel, stay loose, keep it straight!" I mouthed out loud. The trick was to gain momentum and a steady speed, to "glide" over the deeper holes and carve on the gravel when the eventual irregular mound was in the way.

Well, that was entertaining for a kilometer or two, but after more than ten minutes on that road, I was cursing the hell out of my fate. Picture the scene with a drone camera that starts on a close-up of my face, determined, tense; followed by a continuous lift into the sky looking down at me riding the long gravel patch, alone, with nothing around . . . then a loud and full of reverb "Fuuuuuuuuck!" is heard echoing through the whole valley, mixed with the sound of a bald eagle squeak. Yep . . . that was the perfect description of how that moment went down.

The sight of a lonely small sign on the side of the road said "Beaver Creek Highway Maintenance Section. Km 1834.2 - Km 1965.7". The quick math was daunting, I was about to face more than a hundred kilometers with several construction sites.

Just a few kilometers ahead, I came across a heavy construction site. I was first in line. There were bulldozers and heavy machinery everywhere, guys with yellow helmets and reflective vests working their shift, and a sign that asked to wait for the "pilot truck" to come. I sized up the road; it was plain dirt, with a rich raw umber coloration. The reddish-brown tone under the light rain meant mud. A dump truck passed by me on the shoulder of the road. Its tires were probably six feet tall. The equipment was massive, and I had to somehow sort all this out. The pickup truck with the pilot sign came from the other side of the construction, leading a line of cars that were coming in the opposite direction. Every single car was plastered in mud, and there I was, about to ride a motorcycle with no windshield in a pig pit.

The man holding the stop sign flipped it to the side that said "Slow." I followed the pilot truck at his speed. The bike right away started to slide on the dirt. I realized I was riding the back brake. I let go of it and watched my throttle. The rain was distorting my vision, but I was afraid to wipe the visor; my hands were glued to the handlebar. I noticed the pilot car getting away from me. I was going way too slow. I felt the pressure from the cars behind me, but I couldn't move toward the edge of the road to let them pass, since the edge had a foot-high line of dirt left by the grader truck. Another foot-high mound was in the center of the road, so I had to ride smart following the flatter, more compacted tracks left by the pilot truck. The car behind me decided to pass me once the road opened a bit. Mud was thrown all over me, and La Loba skidded abruptly. I wiped my visor and smeared the mud, a terrible mistake that left me with just a couple clear streaks of visibility. The rain kept coming. The cars were passing me one by one and lifting a fan of mud behind each of their tires. Suddenly, the road came out of a wide curve and gradually sunk downhill. "Oh for God's sake!" I shifted down to almost a full stop and let the six hundred pound beast roll down on her own weight. At the end of the hill the tail of the bike went sideways and I panicked. My eyes opened wide, almost popping out of their sockets. My legs spread like a dancing marionette, wide open in an awkward unflattering way, trying to find balance. La Loba wobbled as I was counter-steering in the mud. I let out a tiny string of fuck, fuck, fuck fucks! as I reacted the way they taught me at dirt bike school. Extending my leg to the front of the bike as I turned it, I swung a little dab to the ground and let go of the throttle . . . luckily regaining balance. My heart was racing, and I felt the tingling of the blood running back to my hands.

The road construction seemed eternal, but I started to feel more comfortable with the bike being loose under me. At some point, there was a big bulldozer working on our side of the road. All the cars ahead started to shift to the oncoming lane, well more like the open side of the big pile of mud, but this meant I needed to cross over the foot-tall mound of loose dirt left by the grader truck along the middle of the road. There was no other way but to attack the mound at an angle. I had no chance. The bike skidded severely again, legs went out, and my ass sphincter braced for impact. I repeated the maneuver, letting go of the throttle and dabbing to regain control. I laughed with a maniac tone, like a villain getting away with some bad shit.

Against all odds, I dealt with this dirt version of the Alaska Highway for many kilometers. It took me more than an hour to go through it, at my pace and knowing my lack of dirt riding skills and my limitations. I rode a hell of a muddy road, while raining, on a non-touring, non-dirt bike, non-dual sport, non-ADV bike. Without a windshield, without the proper ground clearance, nor the proper suspension, without knobby tires, nor gadgets, nor the fancy "adventure" bike jacket. For the last couple miles of the mess the rain ceased, and I found myself singing out loud the *Indiana Jones* theme and shaking my head at my daring idiocy.

Heavy traffic, rain, gravel, dirt and mud
A serious challenge for a Dyna with street tires

Many constructions sites stretch for long miles
on the roads of British Columbia and Yukon

A few meters away from the end of those nightmare miles, I found the Pine Valley Bakery, a modest place on the side of the road owned by a French couple. They had crêpes, pastries, and some lunch options. I ordered a cup of coffee and a cinnamon roll. The place felt like a piece of heaven after going through one of the worst conditions I'd ever ridden through. They had a vintage world decor with a few cooking artifacts, a Canadian flag, and an old furnace made of a tin barrel. I sat at one of their tables, drenched in muddy water, sipping my coffee and cupping it with both hands. I let the time pass and ordered a few pastries just to justify my time there. I didn't want to move and was completely exhausted. The pulled muscle in my leg was hurting. I started questioning myself, once again, if I'd be able to make it all the way to the Arctic. How much more of this madness is ahead?

Going back was now out of the question. I couldn't return through the same infernal construction. So, without choice, I pulled myself up and went back to La Loba. I walked around my bike, in awe of all the dirt caked in her guts. I scraped the excess as best as I could and swung my leg over.

The road improved ahead, still a few potholes and small gravel patches, but by comparison, it was a pleasure to ride. I crossed Beaver Creek and knew that was pretty much the last town in the Yukon before hitting the Alaskan border. I was excited and ripped through those last miles in a New York minute. Then there it was, the historic mile 1221, the Canada-US border.

La Loba
covered in mud

My traditional "sign at the sign" to celebrate
completing my goal to ride in all 50 USA states

50 States Club

I stopped at the welcome sign on the left side of the road. I couldn't contain my excitement at the sight of this wood carving, designed with the silhouette of the state and displaying "Welcome to Alaska" in cursive letters. I parked La Loba next to the sign and took a really long break. I wanted to savor the moment, to take it all in.

I sat alone on a bench in front of the sign, surrounded by trees, mountains, and a patch of road, with nothing but a silent breeze and the quiet crack of the gravel pebbles crunching under my boots.

I stared at the sign for a long while in a numbed state of euphoria, contemplating the meaning of this personal accomplishment. I'd ridden now in every single one of the states of the United States, and now this was an indelible fact, a fact ignited by a strong sense of wanderlust, personal drive, and a pair of balls. But much deeper that that, this was the fulfillment of what it meant for me to become a true American.

Just a few years back, I decided to get my citizenship, and then I promised myself to visit every state, alone, exposed, as an immigrant, as a human. I wanted to get to know the people of all the regions of this nation, their ways, their accents. I wanted to open up to new foods, music, climates, learn some of the history, and expose myself to new ideas. I felt loved, I felt hated, I was welcomed with open arms by some, and treated with prejudice by others; some smiled at me, some scanned me from head to toe through a veil of insecurity; some saw the color of my skin, some saw the color of my soul. I wanted to experience firsthand the good and the bad of this country I call home. I wanted to understand America and forged an opinion, my own educated opinion.

I sat there under a cobalt blue dome, with thick outlined strokes of forest green, painting an expressionist landscape of raw emotions. The excitement pumped in my temples with a syncopated rhythm as I recounted the experience of the fifty states journey, a quest for understanding, seeking what they sell as the American Dream, and realizing what it really is.

This journey exposed me to the many faces of the country. Sometimes these faces were expressions of blind nationalism, belching out other people's accomplishments as if they were their own. Sometimes the faces came in the form of vegan-gluten-free preachers, some as gun loving people, some as the friendliest hands I could ever ask for.

I couldn't imagine a better way to have done this journey to celebrate freedom than on an iconic American motorcycle. My trusty Harley-Davidson, a machine from Milwaukee, with a Spanish nickname, painted black, and decorated with Native American ornaments; a motorcycle that had been blessed by Christians, Catholics, Lakota, and Ojibwe; a bike that sparked conversations with New Englanders, Southerners, Mid-Westerns, and West Coast people. There it was, my forever emblazoned view of America on a motorcycle.

When I say I wanted to be a true American, the significance extends to a transcontinental realm. I realized with this trip I'd also ridden ten out of the thirteen Canadian provinces, covering most of North America. I'd ridden in Mexico,

Jamaica, Dominican Republic, Barbados, and Puerto Rico, getting a good sense of Central America and the Caribbean. And I'd also ridden in Brazil, Uruguay, Chile, and Venezuela, where I learned of South America.

But let's be clear, in this age of GPS navigation, Internet, and all kind of information available and ready at the palm of your hand; in these times where roads are paved almost everywhere, and finding developed towns with services is almost certain every forty minutes or so; in these times riding the world on a motorcycle is not that much of a crazy idea. There are plenty of people doing it, people of all ages, men, women going solo, couples, groups, riding on all sorts of motorcycles with a wide array of technological aid. So, anyone who is pretending to sell you the idea that he or she is the modern version of Carl Stearns Clancy is just making bricks without straw. We live in a more accessible world, where even communication differences are easier to negotiate than ever, with robotic translators and where everything you can think of has an "App" for your smartphone. My point here is that, even though these routes have been done multiple times by many others, for me, it still was a superlative feeling of individual achievement.

"Take your helmet off," a stark commanding voice crept through my lid as I unlatched the chin D-ring. "Where are you heading?" I kept trying to release the chin strap from the damn D-ring. I'm always nervous at the American borders; it's a valid Latino thing, and found myself trying to do this with my gloves on. "I'm going to Fairbanks, sir," then immediately realized it was a woman. "Oh shit . . ." I mumbled. The heavily-framed lady gave me a liminal look between angry and jaded. Somehow, I went across the US border this time without being pulled over. It was a little victory for this "brown" kid.

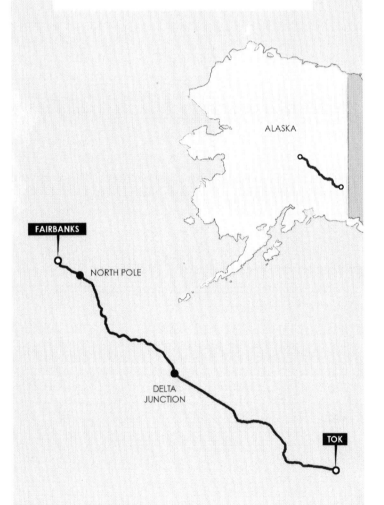

SECTION X
TOK - FAIRBANKS
ALASKA

ALASKA

FAIRBANKS

NORTH POLE

DELTA
JUNCTION

TOK

THE JOKER

I rolled into Tok, more or less the first town after the United States frontier. I was looking forward to meeting in person with a friend I'd made through social media. Chadwick or the "Joker Relentless," as I knew him from Instagram, flew from Hawaii to join me in Alaska to ride together to the Arctic and then down to Anchorage.

We met at Fast Eddy's Restaurant by the edge of the Alaska Highway, which became Highway 2 once I crossed the international border. Chad was riding a white BMW F800GS he'd booked in Anchorage. He wore the proper ADV-style two-piece, black riding suit, and I noticed he fixed a couple Motorwolf stickers on the sides of his helmet. I appreciated the gesture and greeted him with a hug. I know some people get surprised or uncomfortable about it, but I'm a hugger, and I believe that a sincere hug makes humans connect more openly. In any case, I just wanted to break the ice from the very beginning. We went on with an aleatory small talk thread. I guess we both were trying to figure each other out, since we were to spend the next week or so riding together.

It turned out that the affinity sparked immediately on many levels. There's nothing like a couple jokes and a good road story to gain some trust with a new motorcycle partner. We saddled up and took a short ride to the town of Tok. I noticed quickly that Chad was a good group rider, keeping a safe distance in between the bikes and riding in a way that allowed me to see him in my rear-view mirror at all times. I can't emphasize enough how "positioning" is everything in riding motorcycles. We locked on a cruise speed and enjoyed our first stretch of road together.

In the outskirts of Tok, we found an awesome, dry, primitive motorcycle campground named Thompson's Eagle's Claw. The sign at the entrance had the name carved in Old English letters, and on the other side of the road, there was a wood cutout in the shape of an Indian motorcycle that read "Camping."

We rode inside on the small campground path amid dense woods with nobody in sight. There was a small rustic house, a large pile of chopped trees, firewood, a couple cabins, a heavy canvas tipi, a small rusted tractor, and nothing else but silence. The quietness of the place was deep and eerie.

Chad chose a spot that looked nice and flat. The place had some gravel around the fire pit and a generous leveled area with a layer of fluffy moss on which to pitch our tents. We carried on unmounting the bikes and setting up camp. Suddenly, the euphony of a well-tuned engine broke the calmness of the place. A lone biker passed us by on an old BMW R100. I thought, "Well, at least we're not alone in this place. I mean, I just met this Chad guy, and all I know is that he has some kind of military background and rides a Dyna just like mine. Camping in the middle of nowhere with some guy I just met from social media, sounds like a set up plot for a CSI episode."

I took a walk to the small wood shed that served as a station for dishwashing. The shed also had a couple of very primitive bathrooms. The toilets were just a plank of wood with a circular hole in the center, confined in tiny walls, and a wood slatted door. There was a rustic pulley with a cord attached to a hanging disc weight that kept the door closed automatically (genius!), a few tin signs with jokes about shitting, and a spider in the corner that I kept my eyes on.

At the dishwashing station was the rider of the BMW, a young woman not older than twenty-five. Her figure was athletic, more on the robust side. She was blond, her hair long, dry, and wild, and her face was fair with bursts of pink, still showing dirt from the road. We greeted each other, and she gave me a firm handshake looking me straight in the eyes. "Hey, I'm Trina."

The display of confidence sparked my curiosity. Who is this badass girl who rides an old motorcycle, alone, in these latitudes? I wanted to hear all about it, so I invited her to join Chad and me at our campsite.

Chad had already gotten the fire pit going. The wood crackling sounds and the soothing warmth of the fire was the perfect setting in which to sit down and exchange road stories. We learned that Trina worked up on the Arctic roads as a safety and medical official. She told us her ride was a 1983 BMW R100, and she traveled on that motorbike back and forth from the Arctic road construction sites to Haines Junction. She did those rides for months at a time, alone, sleeping in campground cabins. My eyes widened as this kid told her tough stories of mountain construction and rough weather riding.

I started to realize that literally everyone I'd met up in that part of the planet had a master degree in badassery that put my adventure to shame. I thought of the difficult moments of my ride so far and speculated on living under those conditions many months at a time, day after day. Trina's lifestyle literally was a big slap in the face. This short girl was my hero for the day, an example of youth and tenacity, a survivor in a world that for most is defined by a do or die dogma.

Trina's story, her will, and her beat-up vintage motorcycle made me think of some of the boys back in New York; those guys riding their new adventure GS and KTM motorbikes, souped up with all the latest gadgets, with their mouths full of blogs and magazine-induced words, while chewing half a schnitzel at the famous "Two Wheel Tuesdays." Some of those amigos tell stories of how they got on dirt in the Pine Barrens and rode all the way to, drum roll here . . . New Jersey.

I truly love those guys, and many of them are good friends, and certainly almost everyone a much better rider than I am! But nevertheless, I got the giggles out of giving them some shit in my own thoughts while hearing Trina's stories.

Later, the owner of the Eagle's Claw Motorcycle Campground showed up. Vanessa was an upbeat lady, probably in her early fifties. She had a great smile and told us stories of the many bikers she had hosted from all around the world. She joined us by the fire pit and gave us a glimpse of how she ran the campground by herself. The toughness of those fellas had me thinking that just then all I really wanted was a warm Venezuelan Toddy from the original Arepas Café in Queens, but I kept quiet.

I spent the night aware of every sound I heard. Every single twig cracking, and even the whistling of the wind put my heart to race. Vanessa told us that in the morning she had spotted a mama brown bear with her cubs roaming in the campground. Chad and I looked at each other in search of a reaction, but our male egos kept our central nervous system at bay. We just smiled at each other with a "I'm cool with that" kind of attitude.

Chad, having a martial background, gave me the impression of a tough alpha male. In the other corner, I was seriously shitting my pants. I crawled inside my sleeping bag, holding tightly onto my Ontario Marine Combat knife and a pathetic sixteen-ounce can of bear spray. Talking about a false sense of security!

I cross-checked my "tough guy" credentials, and all I could come up with was the fact that I grew up and somewhat survived one of the most violent countries in the world, and getting into school fights and coming home black-eyed in my very early rebel days. That was about thirty years ago, and none of that had any use against a mama Grizzly bear protecting her cub!

Somehow, all the riding had made me tired, and exhaustion won the battle over my fears. I slept deeply, and fortunately, I'm sure my loud snoring scared the hell out of the bears and saved us all . . . you're welcome, Chad!

With the crack of dawn, I unzipped the tent, and we left Tok early in the morning, heading to the closest service station to gas up the bikes. A massive, white pickup truck parked next to us at the pressure washer, then a very tall blond woman got out of the driver's seat, smiling at us as she continued to wash the mud off the truck. But of course! This was a good idea. My bike's engine and the drybag I had strapped on the luggage rack had accumulated so much dirt that giving it a little power rinse sounded great.

I chatted for a while with the blond lady, as I waited my turn at the washer. Her name was Nancy. She was wearing a magenta, light fleece sweater and a pink-dyed scarf. She also wore one of those quilted-style pouch vests that always reminds me of Marty McFly in the movie *Back To The Future*. I thought it was refreshing to see someone so well put together amid the rugged environment of Alaska. Her bright pink outfit definitely stood out amid a world of gray, forest green, dirt, and camo.

Nancy was a park ranger. She had been stationed in Denali for some time, working on wildlife studies. She struck me as some type of director or higher-up position. She was well-educated, with a light hearted vibe. We exchanged a few words as I wiped the mud off the drybag. She politely moved away, avoiding my dirty mess. I told her about our intention to reach the Arctic and then to head down to Anchorage to end the ride. She cheerfully invited us to visit Denali National Park and, with a genuine tone of generosity, offered us a place to stay on our way back from the Arctic. These gestures of human kindness I rarely turn down, as one of the main reasons for me to ride is for the people I meet and the places I see . . . Also saving a couple bucks is not a bad deal. The three of us took a selfie and moved on with our journeys.

The ride up to Fairbanks was, for the most part, flat, straight, dull, and unattractive. But a couple moments captured my attention and made the day. We were coming down from some hills, and the whole view opened up. We were surrounded by mountains, and the sky felt huge. The road was elevated, and it felt like we were riding on a monorail above a never-ending forest.

Riding in Alaska suddenly became real. Over a long stretch of road, we saw the trees violently moving on the opposite ditch of the road. Then Boom! An adult female moose showed off her magnificent beauty as we passed by. We turned the bikes around further down the road to come back and try to capture her with the cameras, but the moose was long gone. I was getting really amped up to have had the chance to witness all sorts of superlative wildlife on the ride.

We stopped to grab lunch in the town of Delta Junction. Chad and I pulled over right at the intersection of the Alaska Highway and the Richardson Highway. There was a rustic, drive-in style restaurant named the Buffalo Center, with a few tables outside and not much else. The place had a couple windows to order from, which were attended by a group of friendly girls that could have been college students from Tennessee. I guess my childish imagination was expecting to see Eskimos and Inuit as soon as I crossed into Alaska. But all I'd got so far was a bunch of blond girls, from Tennessee, I'm sure. We ordered a couple buffalo burgers, knowing the meat was not coming from far, and I also didn't pass on the opportunity to indulge with a chocolate milkshake. Did I mention shakes are one of my weaknesses?

The afternoon passed by with ease. We carried on with our journey to Fairbanks, side by side, with the erratic Tanana River broken into hundreds of small islands and sand banks. We passed through picturesque towns like the one named North Pole. Huge Santas and Christmas trees adorned everything there all year around, even the highway light posts were decorated with red and white serpentine lines, looking like candy canes.

Fairbanks appeared on the horizon. It was still early in the afternoon. Suddenly, the idea of riding on a multilane highway with city light posts became exciting. "Electricity; woohoo!" I yelled inside my helmet. The Alaska Highway beat the crap out of me, and these signs of city life were oddly welcome in my head. Growing up in a "coffee country" had made me really dislike the acidic bite of Starbucks coffee, yet in Fairbanks, I was so ready to stop by one and pay five dollars for their unbalanced brew, in a damn paper cup, infused with some chemical caramel flavor, and have my name butchered by the barista . . . "Tall skim caramel latte for Magooelle!" Ah! The sounds of civilization!

Chad and I rode easily through Fairbanks. We took the Airport Way, and in no time, we were at the Extended Stay Hotel we had planned to go to. "I wish NYC traffic was that smooth," I thought. The hotel was the classic American road inn, with cookie cutter decoration and nice rooms. After checking in, I went to the bike to unload my bags, when a place right across the street caught my attention. A desolated ranch, of some shade of burnt red, with a single large word painted in white Helvetica Bold letters that read: "Showgirls." There were absolutely no signs of anything happening there, not a single car outside, no lights, no "Open" sign, just nada. The super shady, adventurous little devil standing on my left shoulder told me to walk over and see if the place was open . . . "C'mon, bud, how about some titties and beer to celebrate reaching Alaska!" My little devil guy was wearing a "Rainbow Club Madrid" T-shirt and spoke with a convincing voice that came through his goatee. He pushed me a bit further... "Hey, how about a shot of Jack?" ... I replied to him with a "Oh hell yeah, man!" I walked a bit closer and took a second look at the place. I stopped and wished I had a cigarette in my hand to pretend to be casually smoking and not just being there, doubtful, standing by myself in front of that strip joint, looking like a total creep.

The little angel woman on my right shoulder popped up out of nowhere, still wearing hair rollers on her head, yelling all kinds of stuff in Spanish, and threatening me with a "chancla" gripped in her hand, that damn flip-flop every Latino man is terrified of... "Okay, okay vieja... I won't do it, I'll get back in my room and rest for tomorrow's ride to the Arctic, I know..."

I lay down on the bed. It had a decent plushness, and I jumped a few times on it, like a joyful kid on Christmas morning. I couldn't stop feeling euphoric. That day I'd reached another great milestone as a rider. I'd completed riding the mighty Alaska Highway in its entirety. From mile 0 at Dawson Creek to its end at Delta Junction, plus the "unofficial" extension to Fairbanks. I survived her fifteen hundred miles of hell, and for sure, it was the toughest road I'd ever endured. The AlCan road is a living, breathing monster, that lures you with silk smooth switchbacks that suddenly, without any signals, becomes patches of loose, deep gravel. It throws hypnotic views and crystalline blue skies at you that suddenly turn into raging storms without a warning. Magnified wildlife makes appearances from time to time, keeping up a constant erosion of your senses. What's on the next turn? A moose? A massive logger truck? Gravel on the ground? Rain? A bison? A bear? Would the temperature keep going down? Are there any gas stations near? No premium gas? Is there anybody on this damn road? What if I break down right here? In these woods... I felt exhausted but more alive than ever. I fell asleep, deep, weightless.

DALTON HIGHWAY - ARCTIC CIRCLE
ALASKA

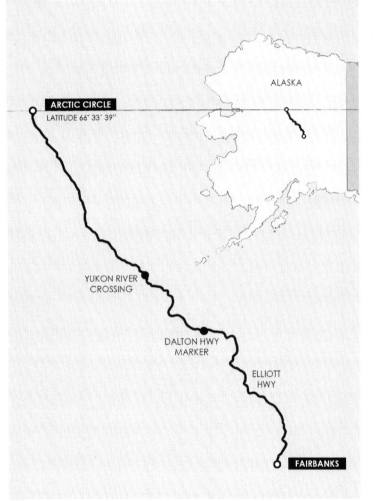

ALASKA

ARCTIC CIRCLE
LATITUDE 66° 33' 39"

YUKON RIVER
CROSSING

DALTON HWY
MARKER

ELLIOTT
HWY

FAIRBANKS

THE DALTON

ROLLERCOASTER TO 66° 33' 39"

"No soup for you! No soup for you! Next!" ... I woke up
the next morning with the TV still on. A re-run of Seinfeld
was showing, and I instantly identified my morning look with
Kramer. I somewhat managed to dry my boots and pants a bit
at the hotel and gave my helmet visor a soapy cleanup. I was
ready. Today I was going to the Arctic Circle.

I met Chad in the lobby, and we packed the bikes. We were
both barely containing our excitement and were thrilled for
the day ahead. Our first stop was at Alaskan Adventure Riders,
where I planned to swap La Loba with a more "off-road"
oriented motorcycle to tackle the Dalton Highway. There we
met with Keith, who set me up with a nice BMW F800GS,
which I quickly named "The Arctic Loba." Keith gave me a
rundown of the motorcycle's functions and particularities.
He also equipped the bike with a "Rotopax" fuel can and a tire

repair tool kit to deal with punctures. I took what I needed for the three days we were planning to spend in the Arctic and left everything else attached to my bike, which I left safely guarded with Alaskan Adventure Riders.

That was my second time ever on an "adventure bike," or ADV, as many like to call this type of dual-sport motorcycle. These machines are specifically designed to perform well on both paved roads and off-road. I'd previously ridden a bigger version of this motorcycle in Portugal, the R1200GS, although I rode it as a touring bike, always on nice tarmac. That little experience gave me enough confidence to optimistically swing my leg over this bike, but while doing it I hit the side pannier awkwardly. "Oh shit...sorry!" I looked, embarrassed, toward Keith, who smiled very, very nervously. Chad rolled his eyes and nodded his head, clearly saying, "What the fuck, man?!" without even opening his mouth.

It took me a minute to get used to the height of the seat, and the riding position, but I soon fell into the groove of the parallel twin and chain drive. The GS was smooth and light to handle. It felt almost like a big bicycle that I could throw around, ergonomically perfect to squeeze with my knees, and well-balanced on the paved turns. It was exciting and different, and I was soon standing on its pegs and leaning forward to feel the brisk Alaskan air. I couldn't wait to take that beauty to the roughness of the Dalton Highway.

On our way out of town, we stopped at a Holiday Gas Station on the corner of Geist Road and Fairbanks Street. We spent a small fortune filling up the gas tanks and the Rotopax containers. We also bought plenty of water and some protein bars and snacks, in case we had a breakdown and needed to stay on the side of the road for a while while waiting for help. I had researched all sorts of tips and information about the Dalton and tried to prepare as much as possible. I even brought a CB radio with me I'd purchased specifically for this trip. I read about the many large trucks running the highway, and someone recommended having a radio to either talk to them or

The Arctic Loba
Riding the BMW F800GS

hear them coming. This was it; gloves on, visors down, and off we rolled.

We rode the Johansen Expressway toward Highway 2 and left Fairbanks behind. We headed north on the Steese, which soon became Elliott Highway. The ride went smoothly and was uneventful. We cruised the Elliott without any rush.

We planned to stay at the Yukon River Crossing Camp that night. The camp was close to 140 miles north, and it would take us about three hours to get there, once we hit the dirt road. So, we took our time and kept a safe pace. I heard that, of all the people that visit Alaska, only one-percent travel north of Fairbanks. That statistic made me feel special, and part of something bigger. I was living a real adventure that not many people dared to do. The anticipation and the unsettling feeling for the unknown was boiling in my head, but my determination to reach the Arctic was always strong.

We stopped to get a proper meal at a road restaurant called the Hilltop. We knew it would be a hard day of riding, dealing with a combination of surfaces like broken asphalt, gravel, and plain dirt. So, we decided to cover the basics before getting any further north. The Hilltop was a simple restaurant, an open space with neon white lights, polished pine tables, and blue, metal, tubular columns. It gave me the impression of my old school cafeteria. The menu had many items named after the area: "Northern Lights Dinner," "Frontier Chicken," and "Aurora Borealis Meatloaf." But the specialty was their homemade pies—strawberry rhubarb, enough said!

Elliott Highway stretched sinuously in front of the bikes, and with each mile the traces of towns, people, and civilization were gradually replaced by the raw beauty and grace of Mother Nature. The day was clear, with a huge sky, brisk and blue. The Elliot was unobstructed and had almost no traffic. We played with the GS bikes, passing each other, testing the speed and handling of the "Beemers"

At one of our many "We have to stop here and take it all in," pauses, we met a fellow biker who was coming back from the Dalton. He was also a solo rider. Jean Luke pulled over on a "round-the-world-proven" Kawasaki KLR650 and greeted us with a bold French accent. He told us the conditions were pretty clear on the Dalton, but we must pay attention to the truck traffic. He said he was too close to disaster when a large logger had appeared suddenly in a tight turn taking the middle of the road. The truck, swerving quickly on the dirt, almost took him out and sent him flying into the side ditch. I looked at Chad and decided to step out of the conversation. Sometimes I just don't feel like hearing those kinds of words of calamity, especially when going back is not an option in my mind. I was doing this, marching on forward, and didn't want my mind being tricked into negative thinking. I excused myself and went on to take a few photos.

About seventy-five miles north on the Elliot, we entered the area of Livengood, population thirteen. There, the Elliot meets an intersection with Highway 11. "¡Qué de pinga no joda!" We were now riding on the infamous Dalton Highway!

My breathing was hollow, and my lungs sucked air to the beat of the dirt on the road, expanding and collapsing to the traveling length of the front fork suspension. The gravel deepened, and so did my smile.

Just a mile away, we found the official Dalton Highway Sign. We parked the F800GS bikes on both opposite sides of the wooden marker. We angled the machines outward and posed for the epic photo that would forever be a record of our adventure achievement. That moment felt real, tangible, and exhilarating. We were now riding on a direct road to the Arctic Circle.

I took the time to check the CB radio. I tuned in channel 19, which is the channel used by truckers reporting highway conditions and traffic. I set a good squelch level and tested the signal and battery level. I clamped the radio to the military-style strap on my Motorwolf Lobo riding vest and saddled up on the "Arctic Loba" to take on the Dalton.

The colossal mountains of past days now became dwarfed, eroded by the violent winds of the world's crown. The shrinking flora gave way to fantastic views of those clandestine skies. An enormous, royal blue cupula swallowed all of the periphery of my retinas. I had a dramatic view of raw deep

Ready to take on the
Dalton Highway

Wonderful miles of open country

granite, an unobstructed sight of the vast capricious reliefs left
by magmatic events of epic proportions.

For the next couple hours, we rode in solitude, guided
by skeletal pine trees, which grew looking like spikes, with
short trunks and a few branches randomly sticking out on

their sides. Somehow, they reminded me of my godfather, Marcelo, who back in the seventies, was quite skinny and already hopelessly balding, but he had insisted on keeping those few hairs hanging from his temples. The Dalton slowly transformed into a dull environment, washed by a brown tint of dirt and dust, of dead bushes and beige grass, faded, with no lushnes or glory.

A little over fifty-five miles further north, a sign revealed that we were only sixty miles away from the Arctic Circle. I threw devil horns with my hands into the air! We came out of a long, right turn to a down slope that met with the Yukon River. We crossed the bridge over the iconic watercourse that felt as if its surface was made of wood slats, but with iron guardrails on both sides and light posts, which were an indication of a degree of civilization around. The ever-present oil pipeline was tucked by the side of the bridge, following the course of the road north.

Right after the bridge, we pulled in at the Yukon River Camp, a very rustic establishment located, more or less, halfway between Fairbanks and our Arctic goal. The place offered simple lodging, fuel, and food, and that was good enough for us. We booked a couple nights there, as our plan was to go up and back to the Arctic Circle latitude on the next day and have a rest again there before riding back to Fairbanks.

The room was small, rustic, yet very clean. It had two twin beds and cheap furniture, electric outlets, snake-style flexible night lamps, and small TV sets for each bed. Absolutely everything was beige, yep, that color. It felt as if the room was wrapped with some old grandma's panties. The bathroom and shower facility were shared and located down the hall from us. All the rooms had carpets covering the floor, so the house rules demanded that all boots be left in a vestibule, which had metal racks and shelves to place all the dirty shoes. I'm not sure if you all know what "waterproof" riding boots do to sweating feet, but let's say we infused the small space we shared with a peculiar scent. Think of it as something similar to the smell of the little cords that tie up a chain of chorizos.

Yukon River Camp
Our home base in the Dalton

Mainly Birch
Dorothy's Gift Shop

After settling down, we went outside to walk around the camp. We were facing the back of the building and were close to the exit. Outside there was a tractor next to a pile of debris being burned. Old tires, pieces of scrap metal, some heavy machinery, a few pickup trucks, oil barrels, and some random garbage was scattered around, painting a picture of the place. We walked toward the front, passing by two large ravens jumping in the shallow grass. The camp was uneventful, empty, and quiet. The crunch of our boots on the gravel was the only sound heard. The place was so quiet that it felt obnoxiously loud.

A few yards away, near the main road entrance, there was a small wooden shack. The words *Mainly Birch* were hand-painted on the front, and several wood panels advertised the place as a gift shop: *Open, Artist at work, Wilderness Adventure, Rent a Room, then hike, then float the Yukon River in a canoe.* A naive painting depicting a bear catching a trout in a river was also part of the little shack decor. We walked straight in and met Dorothy. She was perhaps in her sixties, with a wide strong frame and wild dirt-blond hair. She wore a brown short-sleeve shirt and rusty jeans and welcomed us with her strong hands.

Inside the rustic shop, she had a couple shelves displaying her work. She made all sorts of jewelry from caribou antlers, bear fur and bones, lynx, wolves, and wolverines. The place had mostly necklaces, wall decorations, and picture frames; but also a few photos pegged to the wood wall showing impressive grizzly bears and moose near the campground.

The conversation with Dorothy was friendly, and she was very enthusiastic about her work. She went on to explain how she made her products and talked about how she and her son built a cabin up the river with no machinery. During what seemed to be part of her routine presentation, Dorothy pulled out a photo album and showed us pictures of how they built that cabin literally in the middle of nowhere. As a matter of fact, the best way to get to it was by canoeing up the Yukon River. She said that walking takes quite a while, since there was no defined path to get to the house.

The photos were impressive, showing her and just a couple others building that house with only a chainsaw and a lot of cojones under the severe Arctic conditions. We soon learned we could rent a room in her cabin and spend the night in no man's land, in a place with no road to get to, not marked on any map, surrounded by freezing water, bears, wolves, and someone with a chainsaw.

Chad bought some small souvenirs from Dorothy to bring back home for his wife. In my childish mind, I was just playing a morbid *Texas Chainsaw Massacre* scene as I walked away.

We went across the Dalton to check out the oil pipeline closely. The massive metal tube was suspended about fifteen feet in the air, resting on what could be compared to Australian football goal posts on steroids. It was impressive to think how that controversial piece of engineering is capable of transporting crude-oil for hundreds of miles. It's said the Trans-Alaskan Pipeline is one of the largest pipeline systems in the world, with eleven pump stations that can push oil in approximately twelve days from Prudhoe Bay all the way to Valdez, in Southern Alaska, eight hundred miles away.

I learned that the Alaska Pipeline had a few battle scars, all the way back from the time it was built in the mid-seventies, from the construction difficulties presented by the harsh weather and the production challenges over such a remote terrain to political matters, conservationist opposition, issues with the natives, and a few significant spills. Sadly enough, one of the largest oil spills in the history of the pipeline was caused by a drunk gunman who shot the main line, leaking about 6,144 barrels and contaminating nearly two acres of the tundra. The notion of that event gave me a clear image of the absurdity of the human component. On one hand a brilliant mind designed and built that pipeline for the common good; on the other hand, a drunken mind decided it was a fun idea to shoot a hole in it and destroy the environment.

A few meters away is the Yukon Crossing Contact Station. It was a small log cabin that served as an information center, easily recognizable by the flagpole with the American and Alaskan flags and a board with information about the pipeline history. The tall panels displayed some facts about the type of fish and species of birds that inhabited the region near the Yukon River. The Contact Station was closed. It was operated by volunteers of the Bureau of Land Management, but I guess nobody had signed up for the shift when we were there.

That afternoon the air was cool and easy. We rode the bikes around the camp and enjoyed some time playing with the GS machines. We walked down to the river bank, where the view was incredible. On one side the bridge was perched over the river, reflecting its off-white concrete skin off of the Yukon; on the other side was a never-ending horizon of hills and blue waters. The small beaches alongside the river were of a dense muddy ground, like clay, and the tracks of a few human boots and animals were printed on the natural play dough. I walked for a while, looking for a possible sighting of the local fauna, but didn't find much, other than a few, wet uninteresting feathers.

My body began to feel exhausted. I had a heavy, numbing sensation in my shoulders and my knees felt weak. It seemed as if I had been walking along the river for a while, yet somehow time was standing still. I was in a warping zone, stuck in time. I saw Chad walking toward me, and he hit me with a fact I had not accounted for:

Hey! How about that midnight sun?
Holy crap! I forgot about that . . . What time is it?
It's about eleven pm I think.

We stood there staring at the barely fading light of the sun, as it doved slightly behind the hills on the horizon, underexposing the Yukon River and trees to a hue of purple black. The sky burned into a gust of violent oranges and yellows that kept Chad and me in absolute silence, witnessing the resilient day dim away.

The morning came quickly. I had a surprisingly comfortable rest in the rustic room. We jumped out of bed straight to our F800GS motorcycles and started to load them. We lubricated the chains and monitored the pressure in the tires, also running a general check on radio, gas, snacks, and tools.

The day was clear and on the chilly side. I pulled up my flannel balaclava, covering my neck and mouth. I zipped up my leathers tight and wore two layers of gloves, a pair of long johns, a couple sweaters, and merino wool socks. Chad could've been wearing a wife beater and flip flops; he is made of some tough shit I don't have. Let's face it, he was a man of the seas, who drove nuclear submarines. For all I knew, Chad had wrestled tiger sharks barehanded, had taken a piss in all seven seas, and had Sailor Jerry-style tattoos all over his body to tell the stories. I, on the other hand, just realized there are places in the world in which Caribbean people like me are not meant to be.

We fired up the bikes and took them off the center stands. The dirt was dry with the sun never leaving the scene. I kicked the Arctic Loba into first gear and let go of the clutch.

I rode in the front, while Chad kept a healthy distance. Soon, the Dalton became a succession of hills, every crest higher than the one before, every drop more pronounced. Going uphill I found myself standing on the motorcycle pegs, reaching for visibility, trying to gain any fraction of additional time to react in case of a truck coming our way. Soon the CB radio started to get active. A mixed discourse of voices, hiss, and truckers' lingo invaded the radio frequency. I learned we were in the "Rollercoasters" area of the Dalton. The name was a perfect description of the road. The gnarly ups and downs became a visibility and skills challenge. Going up was like rolling a dice to see if something was coming from behind the hill, then rolling down was, for me, the worst, the steep descending inclines on dirt gave me a very unsettling feeling. In the motorcycle world it's said, "Going uphill shows how good is the motorcycle; going downhill shows how good is the rider." I couldn't agree more with that.

I topped one big hill, squeezing my knees against the tank of the BMW, keeping on my right side of the road and with my eyes fixed on the sharp line that separated the road from the sky. I climbed up standing, stretching my neck as tall as I could, then I heard the voices from the radio getting louder, with two truckers going at it.

Break, wall to wall FatMoose, (beep). There's a Louisville and a Meat Wagon down at the rollercoasters, (hiss), past yardstick 27. (hissssss...)
10-4 WaffleTom, (beep).
10-6 Yeeeeeehaaaaaaaa! (beep).

I had absolutely no fucking clue what anything these truckers ever said meant. But as I cleared the top of the hill, the first truck passed me, taking pretty much the center of the road. A shower of pebbles rained on me as I took cover behind the tiny windshield of the F800GS. The motorcycle shook under my legs. "Shit!" I looked back at Chad. He waved to me, signaling he was okay.

(beep). Break, there are two flies on the road coming at ya. (beep) (hiss)...
10-4 (hiss).
Yeeeeeehaaaaaaaa! (beep).

Well that, for once, seemed very clear to me. I felt indeed very tiny, like a fly not knowing in what kind of shit it was standing. Coming off the crest, the valley opened so wide that I could see the next big truck far ahead, probably about four football fields away. The road was a straight, brown line cutting through two deep hills. I shifted down to third gear and let the bike roll slowly down, putting my weight on the back of the motorcycle. The bike began to gain momentum, picking up speed. The back tire felt ever slightly loose, and my arms were, well let's say, I was a living form of Stretch

Armstrong. The second truck was coming too fast at us, way too fast! He didn't care; this was his road, his work office. We were just taking an office tour. We were forced to move to the edge of the road, still on the incline, downhill.

Bracing for the imminent gravel shower
Dalton Highway

I came to a complete stop, looking at the little bulldog statue on the front hood of the massive rig coming at us, bursting a giant dust cloud into the air. Bracing for another stone shower, I dug my boots in the dirt and held the front brake very tight. With my left hand, I attempted to wave hello to the truck driver and be somewhat polite. "This is just dumb," I thought! But as the truck lost its speed coming uphill, the driver suddenly reacted with a candid wave back, slowing down for us to be safe. Wait, what just happened?

Sure, we've got another bucket of pebbles thrown at us, hitting every part of the bike like a fragmentary grenade, but also realized that being civil and conducting ourselves with manners toward those drivers actually worked. The practice of giving the truckers their space and waving politely at them worked every time. They slowed down, waved back, and tried not to hit us too hard with the terrain. We were vulnerable, and they understood the facts.

At the bottom of the next slope a big tractor was doing an inconceivable U-turn in the middle of the Dalton. There was an ambulance at the scene, and the paramedic was helping the driver maneuver the rig around. I let go of a "What da . . . ." We slowed down and passed carefully around them. There was no sign of any real accident, so I concluded it was a matter of everyone helping each other in that latitude, a matter of survival, a mode in which everyone around here seemed to be.

The Dalton was moody, peeling off its skin like a boa. Mutating from broken asphalt, to gravel, to dirt, as the road moved sinuously through the arctic tundra. I carved through its miles, feeling more comfortable with the bike and more in tune with the environment. I was very much alert, but after so many miles, I was now able to twist the throttle with a thin layer of confidence over the dirt. In the worst parts of the road, I could see the silhouette of Chad's bike, revealing itself through the cloud of dust behind me. Other times, we pushed through the cleanest thin air to ever touch our terminal bronchioles.

We came across a grader tractor going up a hill and leaving about a foot of dirt right in the middle of the road. The truck

Dalton Highway
Embracing the vast arctic views

was slow as a snail, so passing it was a must. Not being able to see any upcoming traffic from the top of the hill, it was a roll of the dice, a gamble amplified by the risk of skidding and dropping the bikes while trying to go over the twelve inches of loose dirt. I heard nothing but white noise on the radio. Riding as close to the dirt mound as possible, I was standing on the pegs, glancing at the hill for any trucks coming our way. Finally, I made my move and angled the bike toward the dirt wall, gently pushing the throttle. The front tire cut nicely, while the rear of the beemer slid, looking for any traction. I pushed harder, keeping the wild moving bike squared, and passed the grader truck while regaining balance. Chad was right behind, standing and cutting through the dirt. I saw his motorcycle skid as well, and the visuals were of epic proportions as we lifted a cloud of dust over the road and just in time before another giant semi came our way over the hill. Another stone shower, another grin on the face.

The few kilometers we needed to cover to reach the Arctic felt eternal. We kept on moving, covering the deserted and homogeneous terrain. We stopped at a small lot, where we could see a sharp vertical rock erected in the distance. The landmark known as "The Finger" for an instant broke the now monotonous view of shallow hills, boulders, and dwarfed vegetation. I used the stop to check the battery and signal on the CB radio, and to fix my dusty balaclava, my beanie, and the multiple layers of clothing I had on me. Chadwick was there, practically shirtless, chewing on a Kind bar.

Let me tell you something about that man. His confidence was such that he could have been riding the Arctic wearing only a stars and stripes speedo and UGGs, no problem. He was the kind of guy that every time he turned his head, I could imagine a fast camera zoom to his face, and out of nowhere, a random, raspy voice would yell, "'merrrrica!" while an enormous bald eagle lands on the handlebars of his bike, bringing him a six pack of Budweiser in his beak ... yeah, that kind of guy. I told myself, "I'll ride with this dude anywhere!"

We were only twenty miles away from the Arctic Circle. The knobby tires dug in with every turn, making a formidable crunching sound while moving over the gravel. Suddenly, the Dalton transitioned, once again, into a patch of imperfect but much welcomed, pavement. We pressed forward, and soon, a green road sign appeared: Coldfoot, sixty miles ahead, Deadhorse, 300 miles away . . . Arctic Circle, next right!

I let go a long and loud, "Yes!" I turned onto the ramp, and a flat lot opened in front of the bikes. We parked next to the famous Arctic Circle sign, still not really understanding the significance of where I was standing and trying to organize my thoughts and emotions.

A group of tourists from India, or perhaps Bangladesh, were standing in front of the sign. There was a professional camera man recording video and some guy with an unbelievably tall and shiny pompadour was talking nonstop to the camera. He was the Indian version of Johnny Bravo, hugging, on and off, the lady next to him. She wore a bright, colorful Indian dress and had some beautiful decorations on her face.

Chad and I stood on top of the bikes, politely waiting for our turn. We wanted to park the bikes next to the sign and snap an epic photo for our travel logs. The man, who kept on talking and smiling at the camera, suddenly turned to us and demanded we shut down our bikes. Apparently, we were affecting the sound recording. We looked at each other and courteously turned the motorcycles off. The Indian Fonzie kept his chattering, almost without a pause. That dude didn't even breathe! We were growing impatient as he started dancing some sort of exaggerated Bollywood choreography. The whole thing was now an over ten-minute charade, and no one could get into his perimeter of whatever absurdity it all was. Finally, I had it. I looked at him square in the eyes and turned the bike back on, unnecessarily revving the shit out of it and moving into his space. He yelled something inaudible at us, at least his mouth kept moving, kind of like a foreign movie badly translated. We rolled in, and Chad kindly told him to fuck off. There was no comeback to that.

We had our own moment recording a little video and taking a few photos to share with our friends and families. I sat there for a while, savoring the moment. My thoughts were hyper-charged with a frantic joy. I rode a motorcycle all the way there, to the Arctic Circle, from my little neighborhood in Queens, New York. I was now standing at latitude 66° 33' 39" north of the Equator. I was riding in one of the polar circles of the planet! I'd actually made it!

Dressed for the Dalton weather, and with my CB radio listening to incoming trucks
The famous "Finger Rock" can be seeing far behind

Crossing the Arctic Circle line on a motorcycle
My face says it all

Aurora Borealis

The Arctic Circle sign is pretty large and has a carving of the planet with a marking of the location where we were standing. Right across from it there was a park rangers' tent. The rangers in charge were very friendly and gave us a little souvenir "certificate" with our names, stating we crossed over to Arctic lands. We talked for a while and waited for the few tourists to leave.

The truth is, we were waiting for the place to be empty, because it was time for me to pay a promise I'd made to my friends, Mikey and Kat, back in Cleveland. Yes, I'm a man of my word, so there I was, ready to make a clown of myself.

Chad told the rangers, "Hey, this is gonna get a bit weird," to which they responded, "Nah, we've seen it all here." So, without much preamble, I hit play on my iPod and the beat of "The Macarena" started loud in my ears. I walked to the Arctic sign and danced a full Macarena, as promised. Chad almost peed himself while recording my awkward moves, and even the damn rangers joined in, taking a "Director" role. I could hear the bastards yelling, "Action" "Cut!"

"Dale a tu cuerpo alegría Macarena, que tu cuerpo es pa' darle alegría y cosas buenas ... "there I was, flipping my arms without coordination, and then came the part " ... eeeeehhh Macarena woooahh!" Where I had to go down shaking my butt ... I mean ... seriously lame.

While I decided, of all things, to dance the Macarena at the Arctic Circle sign, an old Dodge A100 van pulled into the lot. I figured it was probably a late-sixties, maybe a 1970 model, judging by the aquamarine and white color panels. The car became an instant attraction for the few people still on-site. A group of senior fellas stepped out of the van to stretch and take their picture at the Arctic sign. But the one who took the spotlight was a small, old lady, probably an octogenarian. She wore purple sweat pants and bright red sunglasses, her hair was pulled back and adorned with flowers. This was a full throwback to the times of hippies and flower power. Then she pulled a small accordion that looked more like a toy bandoneon and started playing some whimsical melodies. That hippie lady never stopped smiling, and she loved the attention of all the phone cameras recording her impromptu performance. For about a minute and a half, I was in awe. Even though it was kind of cool, I soon realized that peyote was too good for the lady, and I plugged my earbuds in to the beat of Megadeth's "Symphony of Destruction," and life was good again.

Hey, don't judge, generations work in cycles. The guys in the forties went to war and came back as rebels, with their rockabilly styles, cool cars, and motorcycles; then the next generation in the sixties reacted to their old generation by being the opposite, looking for peace and love; then the eighties Generation X came in fury again, rebelling against their predecessors with angry music and obnoxious hairstyles; and now millennials were doing the opposite, being all hipsters, peaceful, vegan and gluten free ... I can't wait to see the next wave of angry motherfuckers to show up.

We left the site and headed back to Yukon River Camp. The afternoon was kind, with open skies and no major incidents, other than having to stop to refill my bike gas tank using the Rotopax containers. We rested at a truck stop called the Hot Spot Cafe, attended by two tough but funny ladies that made very clear their love for America and all the truckers that stopped by. They grilled amazing juicy burgers, and that was enough for me.

Later, we left the bikes at the back of the campground and sat for a simple dinner. We wandered around the place and bought commemorative T-shirts that said, "I crossed the Arctic Circle." I also purchased some pins and a couple embroidered patches for my ever-growing collection. I always thought I may decorate the walls of my garage or "man cave" someday when I settle down in a house of my own.

A rugged man walked inside the small lobby; he had long hair, a wild beard, and a worn face. He was known as "Yukon Jeremy," the son of Dorothy, the local artisan. He made himself present by shouting a few apparent word sounds, followed by a raspy laugh that denoted a "Did you get my joke" type of vibe. I forced a couple "Ha-Has," not having a clue what he had said.

While I was sipping on that extra unnecessary cup of coffee, Jeremy told us that there was a chance the Northern Lights would show up that night around 1AM. My pupils went wide, and my heart raced to that news.

Like two kids waiting for Santa on Christmas Eve, Chad and I pretended to be at rest in our beds. But soon after midnight, we rushed outside. The night was clear, crisp, and comfortable. We were wrapped in raw, natural darkness, surrounded by a remote sky unaffected by any city lights or major sign of civilization.

An emerald stroke of light slowly drew over the horizon, growing into a mantle of green vertical streaks. Soon, the Aurora Borealis made its presence over the entire sky, rendering a hypnotic dance from one cardinal edge to the opposite. The lights moved continuously, contorting and taking erratic paths like the soft smoke of a lit cigarette at rest.

A gift from nature
Gazing at the Northern Lights

I knew right away the Northern Lights were my ultimate reward for overcoming the challenges of the journey. I looked up as the Aurora Borealis circled over my head like a laureled crown of light. That was my moment. I was king. I stood there for a long while, lost in awe, letting the magic of the celestial event feed my curiosity and boost my imagination. I thought of my mom and dad.

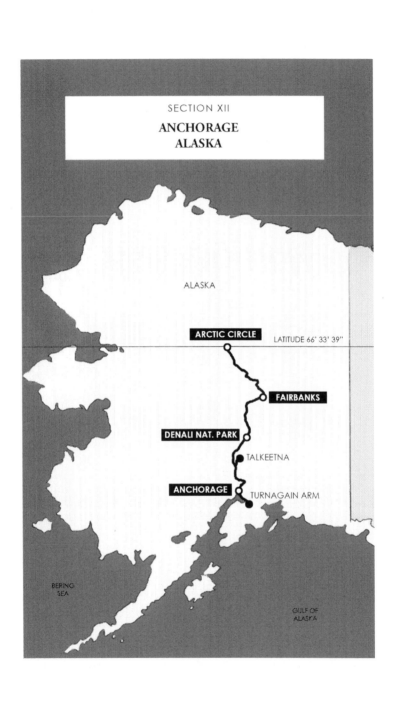

SECTION XII

ANCHORAGE
ALASKA

ALASKA

ARCTIC CIRCLE — LATITUDE 66° 33' 39"

FAIRBANKS

DENALI NAT. PARK

TALKEETNA

ANCHORAGE — TURNAGAIN ARM

BERING
SEA

GULF OF
ALASKA

DENALI

The cacophony of the cell phone alarms woke up our butts in the early morning. After an anemic hotel breakfast consisting of a small plastic-bagged blueberry muffin and some tinted water labeled "coffee," we rode south long and steady, heading back for what would be the last stretch of this motorcycle adventure.

We stopped at Fairbanks to return the rental F800GS motorcycle and swap my gear configuration from the BMW side panniers to my old Harley luggage. I packed La Loba, and soon we were on Parks Highway (AK-3) riding toward Denali National Park.

The road was formidable, but for the most part smooth, with even freshly repaved segments. It sure felt amazing to accelerate hard and lean my Street Bob on the wide turns of that major road. Coming down from riding a few days on the Dalton, this experience was a night and day contrast. My senses could now relax a little, and I could enjoy the views.

We drove past a few languid towns, quite distant from one another. Nenana and Healey were among these barely marked places. Our confidence was high as we rode by several gas stations and small food establishments. The signs of urban life were more abundant than in the days before, for sure, taking a few concerns off my mind.

After about two hours of easy riding, we stopped at the village of McKinley. Alongside the Park Highway, the village offered a strip of log-built restaurants, motels, gift shops, and outdoor businesses.

We parked the bikes right in front of Denali Glacier Scoops, a popular ice cream shop and café. Its signage gave me an instant brain freeze, thinking about who eats ice cream at those latitudes, but the real pain came from its all caps Comic Sans font design . . . which was a deep wound to my Creative Director life.

Chad and I walked around the strip, checking out some of the gift shops, and decided to sit down for a more substantial meal. We found a place with decent sandwiches that helped offset the lack of nutritional value of our breakfast and burned some time absorbing the vibes of the Alaskan crowds.

Two miles down the road we were welcomed into Denali National Park and Preserve. I turned right onto Park Road to stop at the visitor center. The parking lot was full, but we found a tight spot that was big enough to fit the bikes in facing each other. I thought of Nancy, the Denali park ranger we'd met back at the pressure washer station in Tok and remembered her offer to meet us at Denali. I looked for her contact number and gave her a call.

Nancy was not at the park right at that moment, and we coordinated a meeting later in the afternoon. Since we had the time, we decided to check out the visitor center, gather a few maps and guides, and venture into the iconic North American park.

Denali, the mountain that gives its name to the park, is the tallest peak in the United States, and the third most isolated peak in the world, after Mount Everest and the mighty

Denali
The highest mountain peak in North America

Aconcagua in South America. I also learned at the exhibit in the visitor's center about the climbing history of the mountain. The exhibit also showed a few taxidermic examples of the local fauna, including moose and grizzly bears. Denali, which in the native

Athabascan means "the tall one," is in fact, a topographical gem that defines Alaska—raw, wild, big, and free.

After being briefed by the rangers, we were notified that we could ride our bikes to the Savage River Loop trailhead, about thirteen miles into the park. They also warned us about a mile stretch of the road known for heavy animal activity. We immediately went back on Park Road and rolled out on our small adventure into the preserve.

The scenery was fantastic, and we had yet another bright and clear summer day. The road had just a few rolling hills and smooth long turns, making it perfect to sit back and take in the open views.

A few minutes later, coming out of a wide turn, I spotted a very large adult moose. I brought La Loba to a sharp stop about thirty meters away from where the imponent cow was standing. The moose was in the middle of the road, planted, immutable, staring at us. I moved my bike slowly to a forty-five-degree angle, backing it toward the curb. That was my "large animal encounter maneuver," thinking that at this angle it is easier to turn back from possible danger, and at the same time, it is a way to make me look bigger to the animal.

The tension was real as balls. My camera was stowed in the back of the bike, so I slowly reached for my cell phone. The moose didn't take her eyes off us, neither did we. Gloves off, swipe, snap, snap, snap.

A small sedan approached the moose in the other lane. The view was surreal, comparing the size of the animal to the car. As a reference, the leg of an adult moose from the ground to the shoulder can reach six feet, then add the head above that! Me sitting on my bike made me feel so small and insignificant in the presence of this beast, known for its mercurial temperament.

The moose cow finally decided to get out of the road, and we went slowly ahead. The park road opened to a vast valley surrounded by the spikes and dips of the mountain edges, drawing what looked like an erratic electrocardiogram line

Moose encounter
The daring stare of a volatile cow

over the horizon, a perfect metaphor for a place like Denali, where one can feel the beating of the land's heart.

There was an immaculate serenity in the Savage River waters, flowing in total composure down the valley. I felt tired, depleted of enthusiasm, yet filled with a desensitized peace. I walked just a few meters up the river and jumped onto a pebble island formed by a split in the stream. I stood there numbed, away from everything, just allowing myself to be still. I existed; I felt safe, listening to the water dialogue with its shores and feeling the arousal of the Alaskan air inside my lungs.

We left Denali and went to meet with Park Ranger Nancy. We took her standing offer of a place to stay for the night in exchange for some good old biker stories.

At dawn, we got in her truck, and she drove us to the McKinley Chalet Resort for some very fancy reindeer burgers. The place had an open space with fire pits and tables to enjoy food and drinks. This time, there was also a solo guy playing guitar and singing some folk tunes. But the well-seasoned caribou meat was the highlight of my experience there.

The talk with Nancy was very smooth and refined. She was a well-traveled and educated lady, fun and gracious, I thought, while wiping mustard off my face.

We all went back to her house, and she instructed us to take off our muddy boots at the entrance. The stink of our biker hooves immediately became noticeable, but nobody said a word. The house was welcoming, warm, and well-kept. There were a few indoor plants, nice furniture, plenty of pillows, decorative throws, and covers. The feminine touch was clearly imprinted on the place, and in my chest, I felt a burning nostalgia for home and my Megan.

Nancy offered us some tea and coffee, and then she excused herself into her room. She came out later, freshly showered and wearing tight leggings, and a loose, oversized T-shirt. Her pajama outfit in any normal circumstances was nothing out of the ordinary; but for a man being for so long on the road, experiencing solitude and wilderness, it was revealing enough to decipher her body contours and fuel my imagination.

We chatted for a while, burning the night over road stories and wild ranger tales. Nancy seemed captivated by my narrative while lying on the pillow-covered living room, and her attentiveness was sending all sorts of signals in my head. Her posture alternated from lying over on her stomach, bum up, with her head held by her arms and elbows anchored on the pillows; to a side stretch with open arms resembling Goya's "La Maja Desnuda." I couldn't help noticing her woman's attributes bursting through the fabrics and knew this was creating the kind of tension that would get me into trouble.

I concluded my tale in a prosaic, uninterested way, and forced a yawn to retire to my bedroom. My mind was in primal mode, and the best thing I could do was to get in bed and sleep it off. I was certainly tired from the trip and all of its challenges and profoundly missing my house, my bed, my woman, and my kids.

The next morning, I woke up camping under a massive tent, and I laughed at myself with a sprinkle of cockiness. Chad and I were very thankful for Nancy's kindness in hosting us for the night. We both had the feeling it was best to just get out on the road quickly, so we passed on her breakfast offer and went out to load our motorcycles. We found the bike seats covered in a layer of ice from the gelid Denali nights and realized the signs of an early fall were upon us.

The road danced alongside the Susitna River for quite a while. The day was clear, with blue skies and barely any clouds. We rode south on AK-3 for about an hour, when suddenly the mighty Denali appeared over the horizon. The view was spectacular, even at such an extraordinary distance, and I felt the towering high of the mountain. Denali became ever present for a good part of the road. It seemed, after many kilometers, that its size never changed, like a guard on a monolithic stance watching over the land. We pushed on for a couple hours straight, stopping at one of the Denali viewpoints. The pleasant, clear view of the peak was a blessing, as we learned that the meteorological conditions of the summit are quite temperamental, creating all sorts of unpredictable cloud systems and storms obstructing the view.

I took a good set of photos with the long lens, enjoying the color transition from the lilac white peaks to the powder blue skies and waiting for any of the numerous small tour airplanes to fly by, so I could frame them with the mountain as background.

During the rest stop I decided to give Classic Motion a call. That was the shipping company I'd contacted from New York when I was planning the trip. They advised me to call them a couple days before my arrival in Anchorage, and they reassured me that they would have someone to receive La Loba over the weekend. Well, it was Labor Day weekend, and apparently, nobody remembered our agreement. I called every number I had and sent emails to the person I had been in contact with, yet I didn't receive any response at all. Normally, this wouldn't be an issue, but now I had to change my flight and extend my accommodation in Anchorage, which represented an additional expense I had not budgeted for.

I brushed off this setback with the shipping company, since there was nothing I could do until the following Tuesday after the Labor Day weekend was over.

We kept on riding down Parks Highway, taking a detour to drive back up north, about fifteen miles, to the town of Talkeetna to grab lunch.

The small town, with under one thousand inhabitants, has a pretty vibrant main street in summer time, with an abundance of pubs, cafés, restaurants, mountaineer shops, and hostels. It happens that Talkeetna functions as a base for many of the expeditions to Denali, and a flock of climbers, hikers, and bearded explorers fill up the town with life. There's also another segment of its visitors that come for salmon fishing, rafting, or to experience the dramatic surroundings by flightseeing.

We rode a loop of the entire town before we settled on the Wildflower Cafe. The restaurant had a nice deck with shaded tables, but the place was packed, and we were guided inside, almost to the kitchen entrance. I was hungry so didn't mind it. We ordered a pair of the local brews. Chad fell in love with the Alaskan Amber, while I favored the lighter taste of the Alaskan White. We also went for a farm-to-table angus burger and the halibut fish and chips.

We were doing well with time, and at that point, we were only a couple hours away from Anchorage, so we moved outside and stayed, people-watching for a while.

THE UNEXPECTED BEAR

We made it to Anchorage in the early afternoon, with our shadows still on the saddles.

We went directly to the Americas Best Value Inn and Suites, the same hotel where Chad had stayed on his arrival in Alaska before riding to meet me in Tok. The lodging was conveniently located next to a Harley-Davidson store, a diner, and also next to MotoQuest, the company Chad used to rent his bike. Everything we needed was in the same block of Spenard Road, between Lakeshore Drive and Barbara Drive.

We requested rooms on the ground floor, so we could park the bikes right at our doors. My suite was pretty large for such simple accommodations. It had two separate spaces with two queen beds, a mini fridge, a desk, and a TV console, all pretty sparse. I hand washed some of my clothes, leaving socks, shirts, and skanky long johns airing all over the room, which in combination of the typical motel carpet smell, created the kind of musk only found on the seats of the New Jersey Transit buses.

That afternoon we visited the House of Harley-Davidson, on the corner of Barbara Drive. In my opinion, all Harley stores look more or less the same; once you've seen one, you have seen them all. What caught my attention at this particular store was an impressive sculpture of a grizzly bear made of what looked like cut-out pieces of chromed car bumpers. The bear had an aggressive pose, with a raised front paw, all claws out, and a growling face showing its teeth. I found the sculpture quite attractive, reflecting Alaska in its chromed body but also serving as a meeting point for the meaning of "wild" both in nature and in the bikers' spirit.

I bought a Harley-Davidson Anchorage patch for my collection and left, avoiding getting caught in any sales pitch interaction.

That night, we went across the street to Gwennie's Old Alaska restaurant. We couldn't miss the large, mustard-color building with the restaurant name painted as a mural on its side. The inside decor was dense, with a rustic feel composed of stone walls and art of the Pacific Northwest's indigenous people. There were framed newspaper clips, old signs, rusted farming tools, many large animal heads, and taxidermy displays.

Other than the endogenous Alaskan choices like reindeer sausage, halibut, salmon, and king crab, Gwennie's offered standard diner cuisine, with the same alarming size portions typical of North American restaurants. The waitress was as robust as the portions. She was friendly and gave us some good choices, but my adventure spirit was depleted, so I settled on the simple treat of a medium-cooked cheeseburger and a vanilla milkshake.

The next day we went for a ride south bordering the Turnagain Arm. The plan was to reach Portage, a ghost town that was destroyed by the 1964 Alaskan earthquake, being sunk for nearly two meters under the tide level. The flooded settlement was pretty much wiped out, and the only thing left of interest was the Alaskan Wildlife Conservation Center, where people could get closer to the native fauna.

We rode over the Seward Highway, hugging the edge of the Chugach National Park and the waters of the Turnagain Arm. The views were glorious amid the cloudy day. Our first stop was Beluga Point, a place known for whale watching opportunities. We took separate paths and climbed the rocks near the shore to enjoy the view of the waters and surrounding snowy mountains.

I sat alone for a while trying to assimilate this amazing trip, and then the slapping thought of the ride coming to an end became real and haunting. I knew from past rides that coming back to New York City was always harsh and difficult. I knew I'd have to face the daily grind again, adapt to the recycled air-conditioned society of sycophants, the somber crowds in the subway, to switch to that survivalist toughness, and deal with all the collective anger of the city. I looked down and let my bare hand sink into the glacial sand.

We rode southwest, but by midafternoon, we were starving. I hadn't seen many establishments along the road, so decided to stop at the first restaurant that we came across. The place looked open and had a large, yellow banner that only said "Burgers."

We pulled over into the parking lot, up the slope to where the restaurant was. The Brown Bear Saloon and Motel seemed to be happening. On one side of the building there was a large upper deck full of people barbecuing and drinking, with disco music being loudly played, mixed with the crowd's chatter and laughs.

As we parked our bikes, we saw a group of guys with massive and colorful mohawk hairstyles. They wore leather straps and chains.

Cool, we found a punk biker bar in Alaska!
Awesome, we're going to fit right in, man.

Chad turned toward me, and I let go a silent "Yeaaaah," making rock and roll horns with both hands.

We walked inside, and immediately I heard a loud record scratch, freezing the room. It was almost as if we were dropped inside the scene of the "Blue Oyster" in the *Police Academy* movie. Cue the song "El Bimbo" here. I'm talking about a crowd of dudes, all butt naked, wearing nothing but leather ass-less chaps and straps.

Oh fuck! I guess two biker men in leather certainly fit right in . . . don't we?
Not what I had in mind, brother.
It's a gay bar dude, what do you want to do?
Wanna play swords?
Pffff hahahahaha!

So, we looked at each other, hardly containing our laughs, and decided to carry on and order the damn well-advertised burgers, knowing that there were not many other places nearby to sit down and eat.

In the end, it was all good. Those dudes were having a good time their way, slapping each other's butts, like an impromptu drumming contest, to the sounds of Cher, fully auto-tuned going, "Do you believe in life after love, after love, after love . . . "

We just sat at a booth near the entrance, perhaps passing casually as another gay couple, but certainly less flamboyantly, minding our own business, reading the messages on the many dollar bills decorating the walls.

I must say, the food was good, though. Chad was convinced that the water in Alaska had something to do with their perfect onion rings; the crust and the actual onion never separated and had that optimal crunch every time. I truly loved the burger at the Brown Bear, but I can strongly affirm I didn't enjoy the buns . . . *Ba - Dum - Tssss!*

We left the Brown Bear, giggling at the unexpected lunch scenario. It was not until a few days later that I posted the story on social media, and a local Anchoragite explained to us that the Brown Bear was not a gay club per se, but we just happened to be there the exact day of the "Annual Bear Crawl," a known local LGBTQ event.

Remember at the beginning of my story the bear nightmare I had in the subway before the ride? Well, out of all the possible ways, I didn't expect this was how it would manifest itself.

Back in Anchorage, we went to MotoQuest to return Chad's motorcycle. The paper work and inspection were pretty quick, and soon we were back at the hotel. It was time for Chad to get back to Hawaii. All those days riding together to the Arctic created a genuine bond, one that only adventurers can experience, a bond that grew from overcoming unexpected challenges along the way, from depending on one another to go through such tests, and from the sharing of our motorcycle life experiences.

Chad is a badass motorcycle rider and a solid human being I now have the privilege to call a friend.

I was forced to stay a couple extra days in Anchorage, waiting for the people at Classic Motion to get back from their Labor Day break so I could drop off La Loba.

I took the extra time to go around Anchorage. I visited the Alaska Zoo and some local shops; I rolled around the city counting people living in the bushes and burned the saturnine Alaskan sunsets watching hydroplanes land on Lake Hood, near my hotel.

I didn't feel the need, neither did I have the strength to get confrontational with the people at Classic Motion for forgetting about our deal. After all, they were the one and only option in Alaska to get the bike shipped back to New York. Trust me, if I'd had more time I would have ridden my bike back, but work and family life was waiting for me in the Big Apple.

La Loba got packed, with the handlebar bent completely downward to make her profile compact. She was cocooned with rolls of plastic wrap and placed in a crate to be sent on a ship to the port of Tacoma, where she would be transferred to the truck that would bring her all the way back to Queens, New York.

After relying on that machine for all those weeks, I was feeling the separation anxiety kicking in strongly. I stood there watching the bike being taken away from me and swallowed by a truck container. I'm not sure if this was normal, but I got emotional about the motorcycle. I felt as if me and La Loba had became one. Together we went through a lot and came out safe on the other side of a trip that had so many odds against us.

I walked away, with the stench of sweat and gasoline on my hands, and with a heart forever beating in four strokes.

JUST A DREAM

Riding a motorcycle from Queens to the Arctic latitudes was a profound and memorable journey, a personal adventure of cardinal significance, which represented the culmination of several solo rides across the United States, covering every region and every state with one purpose—to understand this country through my own first-hand experiences—this country I love and call home.

Exposed, vulnerable, and Latino...each of these rides taught me about the many blessings and calamities that forged the past and shaped what is now the United States. I experienced how the old days are revered and kept alive everywhere, from the nation's capital to forgotten towns. These rides made me learn of the solemn narrative of the country's history, one of many wars, forefathers, and heroes of the past. It is a glorified prose of events and characters perpetuated on monumental stones that gave me a better understanding of the collective euphoria that surrounds the word *patriotism* in the United States, that inexplicable sense of belonging that is shown by its people, raising the stars and stripes flag on every house across the country. Slowly, all this started to sink in.

On my travels I learned of the extraordinary cultural advances in art, infrastructure, and technology in cities like New York, Chicago, and Los Angeles. I admired the engineering ingenuity in places like the Hoover Dam and the Golden Gate; and for sure, I enjoyed riding the extensive and complex Interstate Highway System. But I also succumbed to the elated emotions that I felt in the wild spaces of the National Parks and the open skies of places like Utah, Arizona, Montana, and Wyoming.

I had the fortune to connect with all kinds of people from different races, lifestyles, and beliefs. Riding across the entire country made me understand what makes America as a whole, which is far bigger than the myopic thinking of many, whose reality is limited to a curated group of people who all look and think in the same way.

Reaching all the different corners of this country showed me something far greater than the American idea of these bubblewrapped groups. We are a powerful collective, made of different people of all colors and creeds, with rolled up sleeves and boots on the ground, pushing forward every day, in unison for a better nation . . . a better future.

In 1994, I came to the United States with a window of opportunity. I had the chance to make something of myself, and for almost three decades, I've done my fair share of pushing forward. But the ride was not always smooth, and like riding the Alaska Highway, I had my heavy quota of roughness along the road.

I've been called offensive names, pointed at with harsh epithets, and often placed inside the bucket of stereotypes. I've been told to go back to my home country and criticized for speaking Spanish in public. This darker reality is also part of the cultural whole in America. Experiencing discrimination or unfair treatment because I am Hispanic has also been part of my American journey.

In my very earlier days as an immigrant, I made a conscious effort to assimilate into the culture by trying to refine my accent and my vocabulary. I learned how to write words like *rhythm, questionnaire*, and *Massachusetts*; and mastered, with almost a poetic eloquence, the pronunciation of *gasoline, beer*, and *strip club*.

And as weird as it may seem for any language native, I even diligently practiced my pronunciation of Spanish words without them sounding Spanish. So, for example, I made sure that when I said *Los Angeles*, it sounded more like *Loss-Ann-ju-less*, and I asked for a *brr-ee-tow* to order a *burrito*, in an effort to fit in.

During those early years, I also learned to ignore the discriminatory incidents that, from time to time, I had to endure. I learned to move past them, acknowledging discrimination as something real, but not letting myself dwell for long on it. I forced such incidents to become ephemeral, to bounce off my cachicamo shell, and dissipate. Some may say I should have raised my voice against such derogatory situations, but for me, these were just distractions, and I did what I felt was the safest and smartest way to keep pushing forward and to stay focused on my goals.

Yet those early days wore out quickly, and very soon it all became clear. I understood that as a Latino immigrant, as a human being with a rich cultural past and a strong Venezuelan heritage, my intention was never to "assimilate" or "fit in." I realized I had never wanted that. Instead, I just wanted to "be a part of."

Yes, I just wanted to be a part of the American Dream, without losing sight of my roots and where I came from. I wanted to find my place in that dream, living in this country that I now know fairly well, this country that has room for all of us, and room for my Latino cultural background to be a positive element, not taking away but adding to the common good.

My travels through the United States, infused by the arcane feeling of being on a motorcycle, showed me that this is a dynamic land, made of opportunities and built by the people who were bold enough to take them.

And here I am, as bold as I need to be for this task, taking the opportunity to write a book in a foreign language, with hopes for this message to reach a bit further, to perhaps a few more people . . . and to tell them yet another motorcycle travel story, but doing so under the prism of a Latino man.

My reasons for this book were simple. I realized the pages of motorcycle adventure stories have been written almost in its entirety by one group of people, pages upon pages of riding stories that leave the readers from my part the world with a very subtle aftertaste of what we were taught in school about colonial times.

Don't take me wrong, I really like most of these books; I just couldn't fully see myself in any of them. As a Latino, I wasn't represented in the way these adventure riders see the world.

But let's look at this a little bit closer. The vast majority of adventure motorcycle books speak of a white man or woman, of European or North American origin, some riding in places like the Amazon, the Caribbean coasts, or far up in the Andes. They describe the lush green of the jungles, enchanting emerald beaches, colorful Andean cholitas, or make attempts to explain our barrios. These stories are often told in what I call a "selfie-stick writing style," as something foreign, distant, and exotic . . . and in some few cases with a flair of invalidated superiority. But for me, many of their experiences are far from being new or exotic. Instead they describe what I see as normal in my life. I played in those jungles and drank my first beer on one of those beaches. That cholita could be pretty much my neighbor, with a very familiar face; and that beautiful morena from the barrio . . . well, that could be just my aunt Beatriz, dancing salsa in one corner of Sarría, the ever-metamorphic barrio where my family came from.

For me, *exotic* has a diametrically opposite meaning, one of exfoliated cultures, of clean water, Wi-Fi, blond hair, and sugar addiction. *Exotic* is living with choices, with safety, and freedom . . .

And now, this is the intersection where I stand, revving the engine of a liminal life. One road en Español, another one in English, with forever memories of an extraordinary ride and a full tank of gratitude for a chance at the American Dream.

But now that I've ridden across the whole extent of this land, seeing the many shades of its fabric, I ask myself . . .

What is the American Dream?

. . . when, no matter how much I've given of myself or how many years I've been here pushing forward, my reality of America insists on reminding me, every single day, well . . . that I'm just a guest.

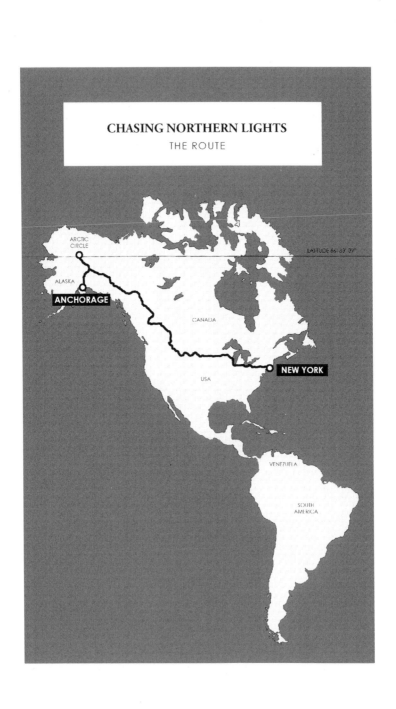

CHASING NORTHERN LIGHTS
THE ROUTE

ARCTIC CIRCLE

LATITUDE 66° 33' 39"

ALASKA

ANCHORAGE

CANADA

NEW YORK

USA

VENEZUELA

SOUTH AMERICA

EPILOGUE

- Total distance: 10,587 Kilometers (6,579 miles)
- 15 states and territories crossed
- Total fuel cost US $437.43
- Tires: 2 sets of Michelin Scorchers
- 1 fall off the bike followed by 1 tube of Voltaren
- 2 pairs of cheap sunglasses lost
- 2,019 photos and videos taken
- Animal encounters: 3 moose, 2 caribou, 2 herds of buffalo, 1 mountain goat, 2 families of ram goats, 9,717,351 bugs killed, and a sleuth of wild bears . . . of the ass-less chaps wearing kind.
- At the time of publishing, I've ridden in 36 countries, all of the 50 states of America, and 10 out of the 13 Canadian provinces and territories.

#RideFar

"There is an extraordinary power in riding long distances, hearing the narrative of your own self, in solitude, and feeling every part in your body holding the threads of your existence."—Motorwolf

In loving memory of

Stefani Sisson "Slickpepper"

1965 - 2020

FOLLOW MY
MOTORCYCLE ADVENTURES
ON SOCIAL MEDIA

@motorwolf @motorwolfrides

Also from Road Dog Publications

Those Two Idiots! [1][2] *by A. P. Atkinson*
Mayhem, mirth, and adventure follow two riders across two continents. Setting off for Thailand thinking they were prepared, this story if full of mishaps and triumphs. An honest journey with all the highs and lows, wins and losses, wonderful people and low-lifes, and charms and pitfalls of the countries traveled through.

Motorcycles, Life, and . . . [1][2] *by Brent Allen*
Sit down at a table and talk motorcycles, life and . . . (fill in the blank) with award winning riding instructor and creator of the popular "Howzit Done?" video series, Brent "Capt. Crash" Allen. Here are his thoughts about riding and life and how they combine told in a lighthearted tone.

The Elemental Motorcyclist [1][2] *by Brent Allen*
Brent's second book offers more insights into life and riding and how they go together. This volume, while still told in the author's typical easy-going tone, gets down to more specifics about being a better rider.

A Short Ride in the Jungle [1][2] *by Antonia Bolingbroke-Kent*
A young woman tackles the famed Ho Chi Minh Trail alone on a diminutive pink Honda Cub armed only with her love of Southeast Asia, its people, and her wits.

Mini Escapades around the British Isles [1][2] *by Zoë Cano*
As a wonderful compilation of original short stories closer to home, Zoë Cano captures the very essence of Britain's natural beauty with eclectic travels she's taken over the years exploring England, Ireland, Scotland, and Wales.

Bonneville Go or Bust [1][2] *by Zoë Cano*
A true story with a difference. Zoë had no experience for such a mammoth adventure of a lifetime but goes all out to make her dream come true to travel solo across the lesser known roads of the American continent on a classic motorcycle.

I loved reading this book. She has a way of putting you right into the scene. It was like riding on the back seat and experiencing this adventure along with Zoë. —★★★★ Amazon Review

Southern Escapades [1] [2] by Zoë Cano

As an encore to her cross country trip, Zoë rides along the tropical Gulf of México and Atlantic Coast in Florida, through the forgotten backroads of Alabama and Georgia. This adventure uncovers the many hidden gems of lesser known places in these beautiful Southern states.

. . . Zoë has once again interested and entertained me with her American adventures. Her insightful prose is a delight to read and makes me want to visit the same places.—★★★★★ Amazon Review

Chilli, Skulls & Tequila [1] [2] by Zoë Cano

Zoe captures the spirit of beautiful Baja California, México, with a solo 3 000 mile adventure encountering a myriad of surprises along the way and unique, out-of-the-way places tucked into Baja's forgotten corners.

Zoe adds hot chilli and spices to her stories, creating a truly mouth-watering reader's feast!—★★★★ Amazon Review

Hellbent for Paradise [1] [2] by Zoë Cano

The inspiring—and often nail-biting—tale of Zoë's exploits roaming the jaw-dropping natural wonders of New Zealand on a mission to find her own paradise.

Mini Escapades around the British Isles [1] [2] by Zoë Cano

As a wonderful compilation of original short stories closer to home, Zoë Cano captures the very essence of Britain's natural beauty with eclectic travels she's taken over the years exploring England, Ireland, Scotland, and Wales.

Shiny Side Up [1] [2] by Ron Davis

A delightful collection of essays and articles from Ron Davis, Associate Editor and columnist for *BMW Owners News*. This book is filled with tales of the road and recounts the joys and foibles of motorcycle ownership and maintenance. Read it and find out why Ron is a favorite of readers of the *Owners News*!

Rubber Side Down [1] [2] by Ron Davis
More great stuff from Ron Davis.

[Ron] shares his experiences with modesty and humor, as one who is learning as he goes along. Which is what we all do in real life. And he does what all the best motorcycle writing does: he makes you wonder why you aren't out there riding your own bike, right now...his work simply helps you stay sane until spring." –Peter Egan, Cycle World *Columnist and author of* Leanings 1, 2, *and* 3, *and* The Best of Peter Egan.

Beads in the Headlight [1] by Isabel Dyson
A British couple tackle riding from Alaska to Tierra del Fuego two-up on a 31 year-old BMW "airhead." Join them on this epic journey across two continents.

A great blend of travel, motorcycling, determination, and humor. —★★★★★
Amazon Review

Chasing America [1] [2] by Tracy Farr
Tracy Farr sets off on multiple legs of a motorcycle ride to the four corners of America in search of the essence of the land and its people.

In Search of Greener Grass [1] by Graham Field
With game show winnings and his KLR 650, Graham sets out solo for Mongolia & beyond. Foreword by Ted Simon

Eureka [1] by Graham Field
Graham sets out on a journey to Kazáhkstan only to realize his contrived goal is not making him happy. He has a "Eureka!" moment, turns around, and begins to enjoy the ride as the ride itself becomes the destination.

Different Natures [1] by Graham Field
The story of two early journeys Graham made while living in the US, one north to Alaska and the other south through México. Follow along as Graham tells the stories in his own unique way.

Thoughts on the Road [1] [2] by Michael Fitterling
The Editor of *Vintage Japanese Motorcycle Magazine* ponders his experiences with motorcycles and riding and how they've intersected and influenced his life.

Northeast by Northwest [1] [2] *by Michael Fitterling*
The author finds two motorcycle journeys of immense help staving off depression and the other effects of stress. Along the way, he discovers the beauty of North America and the kindness of its people.

> *. . . one of t.he most captivating stories I have read in a long time. Truly a MUST read!!*—★★★★★ Amazon Review

Hit the Road, Jac! [1] [2] *by Jacqui Furneaux*
At 50, Jacqui leaves her home and family, buys a motorcycle in India, and begins a seven-year world-wide journey with no particular plan. Along the way she comes to terms with herself and her family.

Asphalt & Dirt [1] [2] *by Aaron Heinrich*
A compilation of profiles of both famous figures in the motorcycle industry and relatively unknown people who ride, dispelling the myth of the stereotypical "biker" image.

The Tom Report [1] [2] *by Tom Reuter*
Two young men set out from Washinton state on Suzuki DR650 dual sport motorcycles. Join them and a colorful cast of fellow travelers as they wind their way south to the end of the world. Their journey is filled with fun, danger, and even enlightenment.

A Tale of Two Dusters & Other Stories [1] [2] *by Kirk Swanick*
In this collection of tales, Kirk Swanick tells of growing up a gearhead behind both the wheels of muscle cars and the handlebars of motorcycles and describes the joys and trials of riding

Man in the Saddle [1] [2] *by Paul van Hoof*
Aboard a 1975 Moto Guzzi V7, Paul starts out from Alaska for Ushuaia. Along the way there are many twists and turns, some which change his life forever. English translation from the original Dutch.

Dis Big Pella Walkabout [1] [2] *by David Woodburn*
A unique tale of travel around the world by an Australian, his Philipina wife, and infant daughter on a BMW sidecar rig. Composed of two "books" in one, it is a mobius strip of sorts, with one book telling of the family's struggles crossing the African

continent while the other provides a reflective biography of the author and the background of his subsequent adventures until it catches up with the other story.

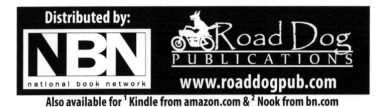